ELLEN LORENZI-PRINCE

DARK GODDESS TAROT

Powers of age and death, sex and sovereignty,
ferocity and judgment around the world

4880 Lower Valley Road, Atglen, PA 19310

Other Schiffer Books by the Author:
Goddesses from A to Z, ISBN 978-0-7643-5796-1

Other Schiffer Books on Related Subjects:
Tarot of the Sidhe, Emily Carding, ISBN 978-0-7643-3599-0
*Self-Love through the Sacred Feminine: A Guide through the Paintings &
   Channelings of Jo Jayson*, Jo Jayson, ISBN 978-0-7643-5718-3
Hip Chick Tarot, Maria Strom, ISBN 978-0-7643-5492-2

Copyright © 2020 by Ellen Lorenzi-Prince

Library of Congress Control Number: 2020930740

All rights reserved. No part of this work may be reproduced or used in any form or by any means—graphic, electronic, or mechanical, including photocopying or information storage and retrieval systems—without written permission from the publisher.

The scanning, uploading, and distribution of this book or any part thereof via the Internet or any other means without the permission of the publisher is illegal and punishable by law. Please purchase only authorized editions and do not participate in or encourage the electronic piracy of copyrighted materials.

"Red Feather Mind Body Spirit" logo is a trademark of Schiffer Publishing, Ltd.
"Red Feather Mind Body Spirit Feather" logo is a registered trademark of Schiffer Publishing, Ltd.

Designed by Brenda McCallum
Type set in P22 Arts and Crafts/Minion

ISBN: 978-0-7643-6022-0
Printed in China
5 4 3 2

Published by Red Feather Mind, Body, Spirit
An imprint of Schiffer Publishing, Ltd.
4880 Lower Valley Road, Atglen, PA 19310
Phone: (610) 593-1777; Fax: (610) 593-2002
E-mail: Info@schifferbooks.com | Web: www.redfeathermbs.com

For our complete selection of fine books on this and related subjects, please visit our website at www.schifferbooks.com. You may also write for a free catalog.

Schiffer Publishing's titles are available at special discounts for bulk purchases for sales promotions or premiums. Special editions, including personalized covers, corporate imprints, and excerpts, can be created in large quantities for special needs. For more information, contact the publisher.

We are always looking for people to write books on new and related subjects. If you have an idea for a book, please contact us at proposals@schifferbooks.com.

Contents

- 6   Introduction
- 6   About the Deck
- 9   Working with the Goddesses
- 11   The Major Arcana
- 56   The Minor Arcana
- 170   *Dark Goddess Tarot* Spreads
- 172   Summary: The Journey of the *Dark Goddess Tarot*
- 174   My Personal Journey with the *Dark Goddess Tarot*
- 176   About the Author

Introduction

Dark goddesses are disturbing, fearsome, and beautiful. They can be shunned or overlooked, as they represent aspects of life that people find uncomfortable—sometimes only when those powers are in female hands. Powers of age and death, sex and sovereignty, ferocity and judgment. Of magic, mystery, and transformation. Of suffering and shadow.

The *Dark Goddess Tarot* invokes these beings, these goddesses and female spirits, that their stories and wisdom may guide us through the darkness they traverse. The *Dark Goddess Tarot* is inspired by and intended for troubled times. Not to deny pain or celebrate it, but to look at it with honesty, address it with honor, then do something about it.

About the Deck

The *Dark Goddess Tarot* is a 78-card deck.
A goddess or mythical female figure appears on each card. The structure is traditional, although several cards are renamed.

0 Fool	Sheela Na Gig	Fool
I Magician	Isis	Magician
II Priestess	The Pythia	High Priestess
III Empress	The Black Madonna	Empress
IV Sovereignty	The Morrigan	Emperor
V Hierophant	Cybele	Hierophant
VI Lovers	Freya	Lovers
VII Chariot	Ishtar	Chariot
VIII Strength	Samovila	Strength
IX Hermit	Baba Yaga	Hermit
X Wheel of Fortune	Fortuna	Wheel of Fortune
XI Justice	Maat	Justice
XII Hanged One	Tiamat	Hanged Man
XIII Death	La Santa Muerte	Death
XIV Alchemy	Brigid	Temperance
XV Corruption	Tlazolteotl	Devil
XVI Destruction	Kali	Tower
XVII Stars	Spider Woman	Star
XVIII Moon	Arianrhod	Moon
XIX Sun	Sekhmet	Sun
XX Liberation	Persephone	Judgment
XXI World	Coatlicue	World

The suits are named after the four magical elements: Fire, Water, Air, Earth. Goddesses in each suit are based upon an affinity to the element as well as the meaning of the card. The titles of the court cards are changed to labels of fearsome, female power:

Amazon	Page
Siren	Knight
Witch	Queen
Hag	King

The Amazon is fierce and independent, the Siren's power is her sexuality, the Witch is a practitioner of magic, and the Hag walks with death.

Reversals are not used in this deck. The goddesses may speak in gentle or demanding voices whenever they appear, in secretive or obvious tones. It is more respectful that they stand upright while delivering their messages. If a card comes up reversed, observe if the position allows you to see something different in the image itself; otherwise, turn it around.

Though I engaged in this work with as wise a spirit as I could muster, my knowledge and experience are limited. I apologize if anyone feels a goddess is misused. I mean no disrespect. The assignment of a goddess to a particular number or suit is not an indicator of her importance, but of an alignment I perceived between her being and the structure of Tarot.

Working with the Goddesses

Only a small part of what can be known about each goddess is presented. My focus is the aspect of the goddess as it relates to the energy of the card. Many goddesses have titles and stories too numerous to describe even briefly. If a goddess calls to you beyond the scope of the reading, it can be to your benefit to develop the connection. Do some research. Begin a practice. Offer tokens of your affection. A few general guidelines are listed below.

When exploring a new power, stay grounded and connected to the other important powers of your life: the natural world around you; your body; your work, family, and friends; your sense and your sensibility.

When exploring a new power, be open and patient. Show respect. Be neither afraid nor presumptuous. Open a door in your heart, in your home, and invite her in. Do not drag her inside; do not tackle her on the front porch. Be present.

Suspend your disbelief. Also your confusion or astonishment. Don't be the person who backs away once the power you asked for becomes palpable. If it's working, go with it! Think about what it all means later.

Still, if you get scared, know you have a choice. You can pull back or move forward.

If you choose to pull back, it doesn't mean the end of your relationship with the goddess. When you feel more calm, analyze the experience. What was the trigger? What was being triggered? Deep powers can be paved over with great resistance, and small steps can get you there when a head-on collision will not. Try again when you're ready, if you still want to then. Another goddess may offer an alternative approach to this one's lesson.

Move forward if you can do so with deliberation and resolve, despite the fear. Often a gift of power is found on the other side.

The Major Arcana

o Fool—Sheela Na Gig
British Spirit of Warning and Invitation

Dare to come back to where you began.

Sheela Na Gigs are grotesque, sexual, female figures carved in medieval churches and castles in Great Britain and Ireland. The figures vary from place to place, but all show an old woman squatting and pulling apart her vulva, an odd and shocking figure to see in a church. Sheela Na Gig may appear starved, with ribs showing on her torso. She may be bald and scarred. Or she may be coiffed, plump, and large breasted. Some Sheelas are monstrous and intimidating, while others are quite cheerful. Whether inviting or confrontational, her image is open and immediate. Yet, her meaning remains mysterious and contradictory. For every explanation of her appearance, exceptions are found. Sheela Na Gig evades an easy definition. Instead she provides the opportunity to perceive another way.

Recognizable in all her forms is her open vulva. Her sexuality is up front and extravagant, and she is occasionally accompanied by a rampant male figure. In a time when the majority of people were illiterate, her absurd and often-distorted appearance over church doorways is taken to be a warning against the sin of lust. Yet, she also appears in secular buildings as well as in places within a church that no human can readily see.

Some say her appearance relates her to gargoyles and grotesques and their function of protection. She is set above doors and windows to prevent evil from entering. Irish folk tradition has it that devils cannot bear the sight of a vulva and can be kept away by a woman lifting her skirts.

She represents sexuality, protection, and also fertility, although Sheela Na Gig is a crone whose time of physical birthing has passed. None of her figures are associated with an infant or child. Yet, into modern days, the vulva of a Sheela is rubbed by women wanting to conceive, and her help in conceiving is reported in the news. She is the doorway by which all humanity enters this inexplicable world.

When Sheela Na Gig appears:

Enter into a new opportunity with trust but not blindness. Open everything, including your eyes. Don't see only what you already know.

Allow knowledge to arise in unexpected ways, like an underground stream welling up from forgotten places, like flowers that burst with the sudden scent of memory, like remnants of clothing from who you were before you crossed the threshold here. Do not analyze these offerings; taste them.

Release expectation and judgment of others, for this world owes you nothing but the everything it has already given. Return to innocence to get on with life as it is. Strike a foolish pose and smile at yourself. Rub yourself for luck. Live fresh in this moment, whether you must cry or laugh or fart.

Release shame. Release the judgments from others that you have turned and heaped upon yourself. Let go of the labels. Everyone is flawed and strange, and so what? Be unique. Be yourself. Be new now.

I Magician—Isis
Egyptian Goddess of Life and Magic

Invoke the Names. Learn the secrets of the Sun.

Isis, or Auset, is the Egyptian goddess of magic. She is wife, mother, queen, protector, and healer of the living, and helper to the deceased. Central to all her roles is magic. *Heka* or *akhu*, ancient Egyptian words for magical power, also translate as sorcery, enchantment, creation, and destruction. Through a trick worthy of a magician, Isis becomes the most powerful of gods by her acquisition of *heka*.

Ra, the god of the sun, has the greatest power of all. But he is uncaring, and the people suffer under his reign. Isis, goddess of earth and protector of her people, decides to change things. She mixes some of Ra's saliva with mud and creates a snake. The snake bites Ra. Its venom causes him great pain, and nothing he does relieves it. Isis offers to cure him, but for the cure to work, she will have to speak his secret name, the source of his power over life and death. Eventually, reluctantly, he tells her. Isis says his secret name while performing her magic, and Ra is healed. But the goddess now holds Ra's powers of life and death as well.

Isis needs her newfound power after her jealous brother Set murders and dismembers her husband, Osiris. She gathers the pieces, although his penis cannot be found, so she fashions one for him from gold and wax (or, in some versions of the story, clay). Isis spreads her wings over her beloved, speaks her magic words, and raises him from the dead. She and Osiris then conceive a magical child, the new sun god, the falcon Horus. Through his resurrection by Isis, Osiris becomes the Lord of the Dead and also the Lord of Life, his green skin representing all the growing things that begin life sleeping within the earth.

Isis wears on her head the solar disk that represents the powerful, severe Eye of Ra, while on her magician's table is the healing, beneficent Eye of Horus. In Egyptian myth the eye is not a passive organ but an agent of action, whether of anger or protection. In Isis these powers of life and death are enlivened by her inventiveness and balanced by her compassion.

When Isis appears:

Try Words of Power to achieve your desire. This is a modern format for a word spell. First invoke the great power, stating the quality of this power that you desire or that can bring you your desire. Align yourself with the power. Realize you are also this power. State your desire and your ability to acquire it. And then state your willingness to give the request to the great power, that it may be fulfilled in the best possible way for the benefit of all.

See clearly what you desire to accomplish in the world, with both an eye to power and an eye to compassion. Do not let your desire carry you into dream or delusion. Clarity and balance draw the power to you that you need.

See what needs changing and step up to change it. Because you can. Energy is flowing through and around you now, available for you to shape and direct.

Success comes through both cleverness and focus. Focus on the goal, not the obstacles in its way. See those obstacles as opportunities to express your power, your creativity, and your ability to skip over or around anything in your way.

II Priestess — The Pythia
Delphic Oracle of the Gods

From dissolution comes awareness.

The Pythia is the Priestess of Delphi and the Oracle of the Gods. The word "oracle" comes from the Latin verb *orare*, "to speak." In ancient times the oracles, the speakers, are differentiated from those known as seers, who interpret signs. An oracle is a portal through which the gods speak to people directly, rather than indirectly through manifestations in the natural world. The most important oracle of Greek antiquity and the only female is the Pythia.

She is taught by the elder goddess Themis, who also instructs the gods in piety, grace, and natural law. The Pythia is named for Python, the great serpent appointed by Earth Mother Gaia to guard the sacred stone of Delphi. The sacred stone, the omphalos, is the navel of the world, the place of connection to the mother. The Pythia speaks for Gaia until the god Apollo slays the serpent to take over the shrine for his own. Yet the voice of the serpent, the servant of the Mother, still whispers, and inspiration still arises from the intoxicating fumes emitting from the ground below.

The Pythia is not an individual but a sisterhood. It is the title for a succession of powerful priestesses who relinquish their individual names in order to merge with the god. In the throes of the ecstasy of communion, she speaks on behalf of Apollo. He reveals to her things hidden from the view of mortal men. The sacred sisterhood answers questions asked, gives sage advice, and utters prophecies. She may also prove a catalyst for change, as when she famously advises Socrates to pursue a path of philosophy. Within her lifetime, within her every lifetime, the Pythia is the most influential woman of the land, for she speaks with the voice, power, wisdom, and authority of the divine.

When the Pythia appears:

Use bay oil and leaf, the incense of ancient Delphi, in your aromatics to increase your power of vision.

Believe in the power of oracles. If you ask, prepare to listen.

Believe in your own intuition. You know more than you can explain, so do not let wordlessness get in the way of knowledge. Recognize that knowledge may arise through any avenue of your being.

Try scrying by gazing into water, either a natural entity or within a bowl in a candlelit room. Ask a question. Then gaze and let symbol, shape, and meaning coalesce from the flow between the water's surface and its depth.

Learn to read the signs and symbols of every day. Study the appearance in your life of birds, webs, winds, and waters.

Read also the signs and symbols of the night, thoughts and dreams alike. Each night, ask dreams to come. Keep a notebook and easy-to-use pen by your bed. Do not strive to be well written; strive for simplicity and immediacy of expression.

III Empress —
The Black Madonna
European Mother of Miracles

Compassion and devotion make the impossible possible.

The Black Madonna of Europe is the Mother of Miracles. In a land where her people are mostly light skinned, her darkness stands out among them, setting her apart as especially sacred. Unlike other Madonnas, the Black Madonna is venerated more for her magical power than her spiritual grace. She appears throughout Europe and throughout the centuries, healing the sick, ending conflict, and aiding the lost.

The Black Madonna in this image comes from the work of an artist from Luxembourg, who carved her from walnut wood and painted her hair and robes in the year 1360. She has a sweet, cheerful expression and a comfortable, casual stance. The people of her church, gathering and worshiping in her home, name her Mother of God, Star of Heaven, and Queen of Peace. After candle soot further darkens the wood and the Black Death is ravaging their land, she is beseeched as the Black Emergency Mother of God. The people she protects from the horrific plague go on to paint her skin black in later refurbishments of her image, evidence of their devotion and steadfast belief in her power and mercy.

The Black Mother of God embodies the primacy of darkness, of the womb. She moves one to look beyond what is apparent on the surface, beyond what is skin deep and what is manufactured. She invites one to accept the full glory of the reality behind an appearance. Her depth encourages one to explore the realms of one's soul. The Black Madonna is the loving mother of a vast but connected universe, and her darkness teaches one not to fear what cannot be seen and what cannot be known. In her arms, faith is found. In her arms, tears and passions are not sins. Her compassion and her strength allow her people to grieve for the pain and loss they suffer on this earth, and then to get back up on their feet to work and worship and love once more.

When the Black Madonna appears:

Assess the situation with an open heart. Success comes when you wish for the best outcome for all concerned, and you do not allow your definition of "best" to limit the good that can happen.

Find a quilt or afghan where you can feel the love in every stitch, whether it was created for you, by you, or by someone unknown who loved the making of this beautiful and practical object. Blanket yourself in this as needed. Let the reality of warmth and love infuse your being, and feel better.

Celebrate creation. Celebrate new life, in family and in nature. Celebrate art that gives people hope, respect, and recognition of the soul in humanity. Recognize the best of civilization. Sense the possibility of immortality.

Pray earnestly and devoutly for what you desire. At the same time, feel earnestly and devoutly all you are privileged to possess. Connect and commune with the magnificence and beneficence of a universe that provides so much.

IV Sovereignty — The Morrigan
Celtic Goddess of the Blood

Never surrender what matters most.

The Morrigan is the Celts' Great Queen, the supreme goddess of a vigorous and successful tribe. She provides for the needs of her people through her powers of fertility, magic, and warfare. Fond of the battlefield, she wears the shape of a crow or raven as she picks over the fallen and prophesies their doom. She terrifies her enemies with the dread appearance of her naked, tattooed army. She leads her warriors to victory against overwhelming odds. Prophesying after a battle, she speaks of peace, "peace to the sky ... strength in everyone." The peace of the goddess is achieved by power, vigilance, and the willingness to shed blood, one's own and another's.

The Morrigan, who may also be called Morgu or Morgan, appears in triplicate as well as in a singular manifestation. She is the trinity of Fea (Hateful), Badb (Fury), and Macha (Battle) to show her ferocious and terrifying strength. She is Maiden, Mother, and Crone to show that her power spans the full experience of life, from the cradle to the grave and back again. She is a great healer and shape-shifter, for all the plants and animals of her land are valued, understood, protected, and claimed as her own.

The Great Queen commands the kings of her tribe to exercise firm and rightful powers in the leadership of the people and the protection and prosperity of their land. Those who do not recognize her do not receive her blessing. The mate of the Morrigan is the Dagda, the Good God, the god of the fertile earth and the father of his people, and a master of magic in his own right. When the goddess mounts him for her pleasure, the earth fruits and flowers. When they couple on All Hallows' Eve at the sacred ford, portals open between the worlds, taking souls from the living or returning souls from death, for her power reaches into all the realms.

When the Morrigan appears:

The situation requires someone to take charge of it. If you want it done according to your best interest, that someone needs to be you. Take a powerful stance. Do not ignore an opportunity for your power to grow and your influence to solidify.

Find good fortune through directed action. Find power in your own person. Know yourself as the ultimate authority of your life. Make the tough decisions that need to be made both to protect yourself and manifest your passion.

Know your truest needs. Know what needs your best defense. Save your ferocity for these. Do not disperse your intentions through petty disputes.

Offer the goddess ale or blood, black feather, and flame. Dance in rings on the earth to build energy for the land and strength in yourself.

V Hierophant—Cybele
Anatolian Mountain Mother

Transcend boundaries through community.

Cybele (pronounced *SIB-ill-ee*), also called Magna Mater, is the goddess of the primal and always primary earth. The great Mount Ararat, the heart of the land called Phrygia, Anatolia, or Turkey, appears behind her. She is seated on a throne and crowned by the city, by the civilization she makes possible. Adoring lions, the strongest and most imposing of animals of the earth, crouch beside her, dedicating to her all of their passion and power.

As do her ardent priests. The goddess is worshiped in orgiastic, cathartic ceremonies. Accompanied by frenzied drums and clashing cymbals, at the climax of the rite her priests slash their arms with knives to bleed for her. New initiates castrate themselves. Their shocking act emulates that of Attis, Cybele's beloved. He is a beautiful young shepherd who promises the goddess his devotion, then dallies with a tree nymph and breaks his sacred vow. The goddess's anger as well as his own remorse drive him mad. Clutching a jagged stone, he cuts away the source of his offense and bleeds to death beneath a pine tree, violets springing up from his spilled blood. Through the sacrifice of his manhood, Attis attains godhood; the individual becomes eternal. He becomes the god of vegetation, the traditional child and lover of the Earth Mother who is cut every year to feed his people and resurrected by blood and rapture every spring.

Cybele's worship lives across countries and through centuries, carried westward with wild processions and stirring music by ecstatic followers into ancient Greece and Rome. There she is embraced by people looking for mystery in their religion and transcendence in their everyday lives. Cybele proves her power to the officials of Rome in 204 BCE. To address the nation's troubles, an oracle reveals that the goddess must be formally welcomed into the city. An expedition is sent to Phrygia. They bring back a small black stone imbued with her presence, and install it with reverence in the temple of Victory. In that year, the harvest exceeds all previous in abundance. In the next, the invader Hannibal is finally driven from Italy's shores.

When Cybele appears:

Use pine in your aromatics to elevate and deepen your awareness. Go to a mountain and feel how it reaches from the depths to the stars, how it is immensely grounded and incredibly spiritual at the same time.

Within a group you can do more than you can alone, even if you work alone as in a writing or exercise class. The group dynamic creates energy that makes you go further and push harder. Gather together to reach for more.

Look for ways to go beyond the mundane in your everyday tasks. Add meaning through ritual, story, or symbol. Add power and pleasure through scent and music. Nurture a sacred space within yourself during the performance of your duties. Imagine what living at a metalevel might look like, where the boundaries of physicality are recognized but outshone.

Create a space or create an event. Plant a garden visible to passersby. Have a party including all of your friends, whether they know each other or not. Invite your neighbors. Call a circle of like-minded souls to celebrate the seasons. Furnish an opportunity for yourself and others to find community and communion.

Dedicate yourself to providing a service to others. Dedicate yourself to the service of a greater power, whether to a deity, a cause, or the Earth herself.

VI Lovers—Freya
Norse Goddess of Love and Beauty

Love is power made beautiful.

Freya or Freyja is the goddess of love, lust, and beauty, the goddess of fire and rich, red gold. She is the embodiment of gold, shining, beautiful, valuable, and magical. She is one of the Elder Gods, the Vanir, and the Great Goddess of the northern lands before the coming of the Aesir, the gods of Valhalla. The brash young gods fall in love with her as all do, and name her the Fair One. Unlike other beings of the Elder world such as the frost giants, Freya is welcome in the new order. She is a magician and shape-shifter, and she teaches the power of charms and spells to the younger gods. She becomes chief of the Valkyries, the divine warrior maidens who choose heroes from among the fallen and bring them to drink thereafter, either at the table of the father god Odin or at her own table, which is equal in majesty.

On her breast the goddess wears the Brisingamen, the Necklace of Fire, the jewel whose power cannot be resisted. It is created by the greatest artistry and magic of seven dwarves. Freya, the Shining One, enters their cave and sleeps with them all to possess the necklace. Loki, the trickster god, desires the Brisingamen for his own wild purpose. With shape-shifting power of her own and strong-armed heroes ever ready to be at her side, Freya recovers the gem every time Loki steals it. She is generous with her favors and direct in her appetites. She loves dwarves and gods and men.

None of her pursuits change her most abiding love, the love for her husband, Odr. When he mysteriously disappears, Freya flies all over the world searching for him. Sparkling dew, spring flowers, and summer sunlight scatter from her hair as she passes. She flies in a falcon's skin or in a chariot drawn by her beloved cats. The tears she weeps become jewels when they fall, amber if they fall upon the water, and gold when they fall upon the earth. She finally finds her husband at the ends of the earth, at the end of time. He has been transformed into a sea monster, but that does not matter to Freya, nor do her sexual adventures matter to him. He remains her eternal beloved.

When Freya appears:

A challenging situation is your opportunity to give more love, create more beauty, and become more divine.

Find success in collaborative efforts where there is mutual passion for the process, the partnership, or the product.

Use the desire of others to get to where you want to be, but give freely along the way. Use charm and the arts of seduction to your best advantage. It will not hurt another to be made to feel more beautiful, especially when you can open your heart and truly see them as beautiful.

Glamorize your surroundings. Plant and bring in flowers. Add some sparkle. Put up art that makes your heart sing. Ramp up the sensuality with luxurious sheets on the bed and the scent of amber in the air.

Cuddle. Get some skin-to-skin contact. And skin to fur, skin to the breath of air, to the kiss of rain, to the touch of the sun.

VII Chariot—Ishtar
Babylonian Goddess of Love and War

Fortune favors the bold.

As the morning star, Ishtar is the goddess of war and hunting. As the evening star, she is the goddess of love. To each purpose, the season comes in turn. Because of her dual role, she is worshiped as both a female and a male deity. As goddess of war, Ishtar stands on the back of her sacred lion, bearing a bow, a quiver, and a sword. Her forward-striding leg reveals her warrior's kilt beneath her dress. Battle is fought for the favor of the queen, and for the right to leadership and power that her love bestows. As Lady of Lands, Light of the World, and Opener of the Womb, she stands for all that is worth fighting for.

Her symbol of the eight-pointed star, two four-pointed stars crossing over one another, has represented the goddess from the prehistoric era through the Neo-Babylonian period. It is a symbol of the union between matter and spirit, as well as the balance between male and female. Ishtar has evolved over millennia into a goddess of contradictory aspects. She is fire and rain, both burning and quenching the land. She is nurturing and she is bloodthirsty. With Ishtar, one experiences the dynamic power that is generated through the ability to harness opposing forces.

Ishtar is hugely popular among her people, prayed to for almost anything they could desire or require. She induces ecstasy in her devotees. She inspires prophecy. She grants access to deep wisdom, wild pleasure, sacred order, good fortune, and release from suffering. Men pray to Ishtar for success in hunting or battle, for sexual prowess, and for fertility in their homes and fields. Women pray for fertility, as well as for sexual freedom, satisfaction, and healing. She is invoked by all for courage in the face of adversity, for protection from dangers large and small, and for guidance, progress, and victory.

When Ishtar appears:

Use juniper, one of her sacred trees, as an aromatic to give the goddess pleasure.

It is not the time to be cautious or timid. Make the bold step. Put strength and focus behind your action and find success.

Set a goal. Give your life more direction. However small or great the goal you choose, do something about it today. Make it a positive goal, such as "take a walk," instead of a negative goal, which may begin with the words "do not." Use your will for movement rather than restraint.

Many things may be at risk, and many are worth fighting for. Many things clamor for and deserve your attention. Be strategic in the application of your energies, or you can lose momentum.

Wear bracelets made of copper, Ishtar's metal, to conduct and balance the flow of your natural electromagnetism.

VIII Strength—Samovila
Slavic Guardian of the Forest

Be wild, and be whole.

Samovila or Vila is the Slavic guardian of the forest. She protects the living beings, red blooded or green, in the woods of eastern Europe. She guards the purity of its streams and the health of the whole. Often lively and playful, Samovila loves to dance. Her circle dances create the magical glades that are found in even the deepest tracts of forest. Yet, she is fierce in her defense of her home and takes revenge against trespassers who would harm her beloved ones. They may find that a stone turns beneath their foot or falls upon their head from above. They may be lured into trackless ways and lost. If their transgression is severe or their attitude uncaring, they are brought into the circles and made to dance until they die.

Samovila is a shape-shifter. When she appears in human form, Samovila wears a dress of glistening white, made of mist and feathers. Her spirit is echoed in stories of enchanted, dancing swan maidens and in the white gowns Bulgarian girls wear for festivals, with crowns of roses in their hair. She can appear as any creature or power that lives in the forest. She may be a falcon or a swan, a snake or a horse or a whirlwind. In this image she is accompanied by a bear, and the most powerful and temperamental of beasts is peaceful in her company. The bear's contentment is a reflection of the well-being of the entire environment and represents the fundamental connection of both naturalness and wildness to strength, health, and fertility. Bear, as the original divine mother, has been known in Samovila's land for millennia, evidenced by prehistoric clay figurines found in modern-day Serbia.

Her knowledge of all the beings within her borders and their abilities gives Samovila great powers of healing. This wisdom is sought after by some brave souls who enter the forest. And granted it may be, should they stand in a circle on a moonlit night bearing emblems of her avatars and greeting the goddess and the animals as a sister.

When Samovila appears:

Use careful force and practical wisdom to defeat your foes.

To purify your blood, eat greens, drink infusions of licorice root, and add lemon to your water. To purify your soul, get closer to nature. Put your bare feet on the earth.

Dance to feel alive again. Forget every step you've ever learned. Dismiss the demands of music. Move because the breeze is sweet. Move with strength and grace in each simple, living moment, at any and every opportunity.

Imitate the way an animal you love moves. Develop your connection with this animal through dance, art, knowledge, appreciation, and experience. Invite the spirit of this animal to become your totem and your friend, and feel new strength sing in your blood.

Imitate Samovila's stance of power and prepare to defend against those who would use you and yours for immoral purposes. Do not be lured by greed or lust into betraying your values.

IX Hermit—Baba Yaga
Russian Witch of the Woods

Keep going, knowing the journey does not end.

Baba Yaga is the fearsome Russian witch of the woods, with iron teeth, bony legs, and a nose so long it rattles the roof of her hut when she snores. She lives in a hut in the trackless forest. Her home has a personality of its own—its windows are eyes, and it moves about on giant chicken legs. It can follow wherever Baba Yaga chooses to wander in her northern woods. She travels bent and perched inside a giant mortar, pushing herself across the forest floor or flying and stirring up the skies with her large pestle. Her other hand holds a birch broom to erase the traces of her passing. She is reclusive, with no wish to be disturbed, content as she is with the company of spirits and her faithful, mysterious servants: the bodiless hands she calls soul friends, and her beloved horsemen, the white, the red, and the black, whom she calls Bright Dawn, Red Sun, and Dark Midnight. Her powers are earthy and old and as encompassing as time.

She may be encountered by a hero undertaking a journey, though her hut is so hidden it is hard to find, unless a magical doll or thread shows the way. When they enter her home, they live or die by what they say and do. When they enter for the sake of love or virtue, when they are honest and true to their heart and their purpose—and perform whatever impossible task Baba Yaga sets them to test their purity and intent—they may be able to go on their way without being baked in her stone oven and eaten. They may even be given magical gifts to help them fulfill their original quest.

Peoples living within the northern forests of Russia and Finland honor Baba Yaga with stone statues set on tree stumps, often with little huts full of tiny offerings. The statues are asked for advice, and then the petitioner hushes to listen for the words of the Wisewoman of the Woods.

When Baba Yaga appears:

What appear as odd distractions or challenges can bring you to a rewarding place. Trust the momentum of your soul's journey. Do not rethink each step. Do not judge the worth of an experience until you have undergone it.

Virtue and honesty may not prevail in sophisticated places, but they do in the forests. Know where to find authenticity. Turn away from false spirits that do not lead you true.

Within nature, within your mind, seek out the still and sacred places where magic is heard and felt and seen. Spend enough time to feel this as an integral part of who you are.

Learn through experience over instruction. Follow intuition over authority.

Ask invisible friends to be your companions. This is a good time to explore or deepen relationships with unseen beings.

X Wheel of Fortune—Fortuna
European Goddess of Fate and Fortune

The high fall and the low ascend.

The goddess Fortuna at her wheel appears in art from ancient Rome through the Middle Ages in Europe and into the modern age in every land touched by the old empire. Boethius describes the goddess in his popular and enduring sixth-century work *The Consolation of Philosophy*. He writes as he awaits his execution during the fall of the Roman Empire, understanding he has had his time in the sun, knowing as well it is not merely his life that is coming to an end—Fortune is Fate at the end, Fortune always has ups and downs, and Fate will have the last word. His goddess of Fortune speaks thus, "This is my art, this the game I never cease to play. I turn the wheel that spins. I delight to see the high come down and the low ascend."

Fortuna, the goddess of chance and of the lot, is far more interested in change than fairness. She wears a pair of golden wings, symbolizing a separation from mundane concerns, and an expression that looks far beyond the struggles occurring in front of her. Rich and poor alike climb and cling, but her wheel keeps going around, and no one rides forever.

In Rome, separate altars are built for both her faces, for the two sides of luck, Mala Fortuna and Bona Fortuna. She is an oracular goddess, often consulted about the future she foresees and the present she holds in her hands. More often she is entreated to be kind and bestow her favors more liberally to one who pleas most sweetly.

More than a gambler's fixation, Fortuna's wheel is also a chariot's means of motion and a ship's helm for direction, for those who trust Fate and Fortune to be their guide.

When Fortuna appears:

Roll with the punches. If things are falling down, use the momentum to help you spring back. Someone trying to land on their feet and stabilize immediately is not back in action sooner than someone who takes the tumble with knowledge and grace. A fall is part of the path, and the path is ever changing.

If things are looking up, take the ride for all its worth. Enjoy the pleasures of the moment. Be generous with your good fortune. But also use this time to build on what can aid and sustain you when harder times come, whether it is experience and wisdom or something more concrete, such as a home, a vehicle, or a savings plan.

There is an old story of a young farmer who broke his leg at harvest time, but when an army swept through he was not conscripted. Good or bad luck is not always as it appears. Remember that Fortuna sees farther than you do.

To turn your luck around: Wear your clothes inside out for a day. Part your hair on the other side. Stand up and turn around three times. Give away the last coins in your pocket.

XI Justice — Maat
Egyptian Goddess of Truth and Justice

Speak only what is true.

Maat or Ma'at is the ancient Egyptian goddess of truth, balance, law, morality, and justice. All of these ideals are one and the same in her. The ancient Egyptians deeply believed in the holiness, unity, and equilibrium of the universe. The goddess Maat sets and continually maintains the order of the stars and all the worlds, lest the powers of chaos overtake creation. She stands behind the sun, Ra, as the guiding principle of life. Humanity participates in this divine, cosmic harmony through correct civic and ritual behavior.

The most important expression of the veneration of the goddess is not within a temple dedicated to her, for those are comparatively rare. It is the king's ritual presentation of a small figure of Maat in the temples of other gods, particularly in the temples of Amun, Ra, and Ptah, the most-ancient gods of creation. With this offering, the king vows to work toward preserving order and justice on their behalf.

Maat is depicted as a woman wearing a feather in her hair. She may have outstretched wings or hold a scepter for power, an ankh for life, or a scale for judgment. In the Papyrus of Ani, known today as the Book of the Dead, she becomes the scale itself. Within the Hall of Truths, she weighs the souls of the deceased as they enter the underworld. The human heart, where the soul has its home, is balanced against her single sacred feather. A light heart, one free from wrongdoing, may continue on the journey toward paradise. The unworthy heart is devoured by the ferocious monster of the underworld, the goddess Ammut.

Chapter or spell 125 of the Papyrus of Ani lists forty-two Declarations of Purity, the so-called Negative Confessions. This is a magical spell for the absolution of the soul of the deceased. Through the power of words and the magic of writing, transgressions against harmony can be cleared off the cosmic record and enable the soul to pass the judgment of Maat. Some of these declarations: I have caused none to weep. I have not eaten the heart (through regret). I am not a stirrer of strife. I have never stopped the flow of water. In a land where crops grow exclusively through irrigation, this last is more than metaphoric. In another text from the New Kingdom era, the Book of the Cow of Heaven, one is advised to paint a figure of Maat on one's tongue. This ritual ensures that the individual will speak only what is true. For the magician, it allows what is spoken to become true.

When Maat appears:

Evaluate your relationships, whether intimate or public, for right conduct. Where cruelty, falsehood, entitlement, or servility exists, realize how your heart is eroded by these actions.

An opportunity exists for your voice to be heard. An opportunity exists for you to be a voice of justice.

Maintaining calm and creating order is beneficial. Do not invite chaos into your life.

Speak aloud what you wish for. Write down your confession. Draw up a contract. There is power to be gained in formal declarations of intent.

To reveal the truth of an unjust situation, set a light in a window, using an oil lamp or a candle scented with frankincense or myrrh. Gaze at the flame and scry for how the inequity may come to light to be redressed.

XII Hanged One—Tiamat
Babylonian Goddess of the Deep

What has been lost lives in hidden places.

Tiamat is the Babylonian goddess of the deep, the power and being of the vast salt waters of the seas. She appears in ancient stories as a bloated dragon, a terrible serpent, a monster of chaos. She also appears as a caring and generous mother. Tiamat is the mother of the gods, the mother of all existence. Her reality extends beyond the dawn of time into the realm of eternity. She is the primordial sea, where hidden life teems and where all is ultimately dissolved. She is the great ocean void that surrounds and holds the earth and all its seas.

In the beginning, Tiamat mates with Apsu, the god of the freshwater abyss that lies beneath the earth. The sweet water rising and mingling with salt brings the younger gods into being. The brash young ones grow pesky underfoot and eventually rebel against their father. War erupts and Apsu is killed. Tiamat seeks revenge thereafter, grieving for her beloved, for her children, for a world of wholeness that is lost forever. Added to her tears are her birth waters as she brings forth monsters, giant snakes, hooded dragons, and hybrid human-animal demons, to fight in the war.

Finally, Tiamat herself faces the child and champion of the young gods, Marduk the storm god, in single combat. She casts spells of deep magic, but Marduk catches her in a net, batters her with winds, and finally cuts her apart. The body of the goddess becomes the universe, one half the dome of heaven, one half the fundament of earth. The waters of the world pour forth from her. Her eyes become the sources of the great rivers. Her tears are the ever-flowing, life-giving Tigris and Euphrates. Her sacrifice creates the cradle of civilization.

Although at the new year Marduk's followers celebrate the hero's destruction and control of primeval chaos, the wise and the lost know that the Ancestress, the Great Dragoness, still lives in the deep.

When Tiamat appears:

Surrender as you must to the inexorable forces of the time, but remember who you are. Hold to the scent, the thread, the stream. Follow it as deep as you need, as far as you can, and remember.

Intuition is information that wells up from within, from your deepest, truest source. Keeping your attention focused in the upper mind cuts you off from this source of knowledge. Archetypes live though the stories about them change. Learn the language they speak throughout time. Look at the symbols, the patterns, the resemblances. See the spirit who has been with you all along.

Look at things from a different point of view: as if you were a god, as if you were a dragon, as if you were completely whole, as if your heart were somewhere far away.

XIII Death—La Santa Muerte

Mexican Goddess of Death

Death is the destiny of life.

La Santa Muerte, Saint Death or Holy Death, is the beloved death goddess of Mexico and the United States. Once the Mictecacihuatl, the Aztec Lady of the Land of the Dead and the Protector of Souls, under European influence she appears now as a grim reaper with scythe and robe. She wears a necklace of gold coins and holds a globe of the world to represent her worldly power. She reigns over the destinies of life as well as the moments of death, for she holds all life's ends in her hands. Her people most commonly petition La Santa Muerte for a good destiny, a peaceful death.

Most Holy Death, La Santísima Muerte, oversees the many needs of her people. She hears rituals for justice in court cases, for protection from enemies, for success in business or in love, and for the removal of curses. Her people also ask to know the truth of things unseen. They offer her food and flowers; red, black, and white candles; tobacco; and tequila. They know the Lady may grant any prayer. In providing a good life, in providing a good death, she feeds herself as well. For La Santísima is the hard and practical earth, the one who builds and sustains life by gripping, holding, and processing the dead.

The robes of La Santa Muerte can be red, white, or black. She manifests herself as a trinity, as three distinct faces of Death: La Blanca, La Roja, and La Negra. La Blanca, the White Lady, is the gentlest, the most protective of her children, and the most often petitioned. La Roja, the Red One, the passionate one, is invoked for purposes of love, lust, anger, and risk. The Black One, the most mysterious and dangerous of the three, is called upon only in the direst of circumstances. Only when one is truly facing the end.

When La Santa Muerte appears:

See the truth of the habits that get in the way of building a better life for yourself. Tear down the walls and slay the inner demons. Ask for knowledge and strength. Do not give up or lose faith that it can be done.

A relationship is at an end, a relationship that may be between you and another, or between you and your previous self. If it is right to say goodbye, say it and do not look back. If it is sad to say goodbye, first offer your tears for what has been lost.

Bring an end to negative actions and energies directed toward you by another. Do not engage, but strengthen your position as much as possible and take your petition to a higher authority.

Grow a pot of La Santa Muerte's sacred aloe, a spiny plant of the arid desert that is full of moisture and healing within.

To offer your life to the goddess and be under her protection does not mean her scythe may not fall upon your neck at any moment. Awareness of death must come with both trust and acceptance. And gratitude for the gift of each moment.

XIV Alchemy—Brigid
Irish Goddess of Craft, Art, and Healing

Fire purifies. Water restores.

Brigid, "Bright Arrow," is the Irish goddess of craft, poetry, and healing. Powerful and approachable, she is beloved by the people of the Misty Isles, and her popularity has given her many names and many voices throughout the centuries. Brigid gives her people knowledge of the arts that are wise, practical, and inspired. She is a goddess of fire, and her flame burns in Kildare and in hearths throughout her lands. She is a goddess of water, and her sacred wells dot the countryside. Her vessel is the cauldron. Her vessel is the forge. A triple goddess, she is the one and the other and then something more, something new that arises from the union.

As the goddess of smithcraft, she structures and sanctifies a relationship with primal fire, asking for strength and intelligence in return. The smith, the craftsperson, takes the elements into his or her hands to forge something new, useful, and meaningful. Brigid inspires her people to invent and build the artifacts of culture.

As goddess of poetry, Brigid inspires and preserves the oral teachings of her people, the wisdom in songs and tales. She is the muse of bards and of artists of all kinds. She is the cauldron of beauty, history, and creation in which they dip.

As goddess of healing, she is the patroness of druids, healers, and wisewomen, those understanding herbal and medical lore, and those with the knowledge and gifts of divination and prophecy.

Although she is the Bright One, Brigid weds a dark figure, King Bress, whose progenitors are the Fomorii, the spirits of the evil dead. Together they have a trinity of sons: Day, Light, and Life. Brigid wails after finding her beloved son dead on the battlefield, initiating the practice of keening for grief and protest, a sacred gift of expression and power during dark days.

When Brigid appears:

The situation is improved by adding a combination of skill and attention.

Difficult feelings require expression, not suppression. Keen your grief. Speak your rage. Forge your purpose. Pull the personal pain out of your soul for the fuel to make something tangible from it. Show the world what it is, and what it should be.

Bring your regular practice to another level through the implementation of a grander vision and a deeper desire. Find inspiration in the elemental world. Observe the will and the dance of Fire. Sense the mystery and the wisdom of Water.

Bring balance into your life. If you feel too withdrawn, add activity. Stretch your legs, your arms, your neck, your mind. If you feel too busy, add quietude. Turn off the music, the program, the monologue, the lights. Balance is not a static but a living process. It is a measured flow, a graceful dance performed every day.

XV Corruption — Tlazolteotl
Aztec Goddess of Filth and Purification

Disease is cruel but not irredeemable.

Present at the dawn of the world, Tlazolteotl (pronounced *tlah-SOL-tay-oht*) is the Mother of the Aztec Gods. Her name is from the ancient Nahuatl language: *tlazolli* signifies filth, refuse, excrement, sin, vice, and all that is dirty and deteriorated, and *teotl* represents a deity. She is called the Sin Eater, the Mother of Midnight, Death by Lust, and She of Two Faces. She is the contrary-natured Aztec and Toltec goddess of filth and purification, of fertility and disease, of prostitutes and midwives. In one hand she hold a cob of maize for the powers of life, in the other a rattle, symbolic of the scourge of illness. Her mouth and chin are black from chewing bitumen, a smelly, sticky, natural form of petroleum used for paint. Unmarried women of her people chew bitumen to advertise their fertility and availability.

When Tlazolteotl takes possession of a person, she causes them to lose their senses, fall into convulsions, break out in pustules, spit blood, and commit acts of evil. She twists minds and bodies with ugliness and suffering. Yet, she is also the goddess of purification, whose sacred rites include taking a steam bath to sweat out pollutants. She forgives sin and cleanses its stain upon the soul. She protects from the evildoing of others. She addresses suffering and provides healing, relief, and revolution.

Like life in the material world, Tlazolteotl has a challenging, complex reality. She is a fourfold goddess, appearing as a sisterhood in the four stages of life. Xocotzin is the Youngest Sister, the innocent and cruel child. Tlaco, Middle Sister, is the adventurous, sexually active young woman. Teicu, Younger Sister, is the witch goddess who devours the sins of humanity, purifies the souls of those who confess, and aids in childbirth. Tiacapan, the First Born, is the oldest sister and the harshest, the one who brings disease and destruction and then grants or withholds cure and change and the opportunity to move on.

When Tlazolteotl appears:

Basic realities include unpleasant tasks and distasteful choices. Avoidance of these tasks complicates them further. Choices of convenience catch up with you when you stop running.

Be careful, be mindful, lest you open yourself to accident and sickness.

Deal with the nitty-gritty of your life, whether of the everyday or more esoteric kind. Deal with your dirt, your pain, your compulsions, your delusions. Give into temptation, or work to cleanse it from your life, but acknowledge what drives you, what hurts you, what twists you, what binds you.

A shadow covers the situation. The participants have hidden agendas. Get clarity on details, motive, and accountability. Be sure you understand your own motives as well.

Pettiness accumulates. Do not let it fester. Old wounds ache. Do not let them dominate the present.

XVI Destruction—Kali
Hindu Goddess of the End of Time

All the world changes.

Kali is the Hindu destroyer of worlds, and the goddess of cemeteries. She is Black Mother Time. Her skin is the blue or black of the endless eternal void. Her necklace of heads stands for the severance of the ego and of ignorance. Her skirt of dismembered limbs represents humanity's impotence in the face of her awesome reality. Her hair is wild, untamed, billowing from her like a cloak of dark fire. Skulls tumble from her hands, for even Death falls before her. The eighteenth-century Bengal poet Ramprasad writes:

When Death

Grabs you by the hair,

Call out: Kali, Kali—

Then what can He do?

Kali is birthed from the brow, from the concentration of the goddess Durga in her need. Demons overrun the world, and even fierce Durga cannot slay them all. When the demon lord is wounded, new spawn arise from every drop of his blood that touches the ground. Kali vanquishes him and saves the world by holding him above the earth and drinking his blood as it falls.

But her force cannot be stopped once invoked. Kali, the power of time that leads all to ruin, thrives on blood. Drunk on slaughter, she dances, growing ever more wanton, crushing all beneath her furious steps. Only when Shiva, Lord of the Dance of Life, puts himself beneath her feet does she awaken and slow her wild rush. Someday she will resume the dance that ends the world. When she has destroyed everything, Kali will be the void out of time from which new worlds are born.

Kali gives her name to the great city of Calcutta (Kali Ghat, "Steps of Kali"), her temple city and the center of her worship where goat blood is spilled for her pleasure. Yet, Kali is beloved by her people, for she allows them to move beyond fear. Facing the annihilation of all that is beloved and familiar, and yet persevering in their devotion and humble understanding, sets her people free.

When Kali appears:

Pray that Kali will be kind. Offer her red flowers and red foods on dark, new-moon nights. Offer her theater and fireworks and charred flesh. A blood sacrifice means giving up something important, something not easy to give, something with life and meaning.

Illusions, whether cherished or not, shatter. Your personal reality crumbles along with it. Ride it out as best you can. Do not cling to any individual, scattering piece but focus on understanding the intangibles of the situation, the shift of energy that has occurred. Then you will know best how to proceed.

Do not evade dealing with something difficult, lest the crushing continue. Destruction can be slow and grinding as well as violent and sudden. Get on with it and get out from under or be dust.

XVII Stars — Spider Woman
Hopi Goddess of Thought and Creation

Small things hold the Earth to Heaven.

In the high desert of the American Southwest, Spider Woman is revered as the creator of the world and benefactor of her people. In the mesas of the Hopi, her name is Kokyangwuti (pronounced similar to *koh-kyang-woo-tee*). For the Pueblo, she is S'ts'tsi'naku (*tse-che-nako*). She is called Thinking Woman, Old Spider Woman, and Grandmother Spider. Although she is ancient, her power of renewal is shown through her hair, dressed in the whorls of the squash blossom, the symbol of fertility. She draws light and life from darkness.

Spider Woman creates through her thought, through her vision, through the powers of clarity and consciousness, through the powers of a universe that sings inside her. She creates the stars by spinning a web, lacing it with the precious dew, and tossing it into the sky. She creates the stars to shine upon her people in the darkest night. She arranges the constellations to show her people there is meaning in creation. A single star in the sky may appear to be a small thing but be significant in its relation to another, through the patterns they make together and in the feelings the expanse of a starry night evokes.

In the darkness in the beginning of time, Spider Woman is told she is too small and weak to help, yet through intelligence, persistence, and belief, she travels to and returns safely from the Lake of Fire. She succeeds in bringing light and warmth into the world where more-imposing animals try and fail. In another tale, she keeps the rising sky from leaving the world entirely by spinning web lines day and night to tie heaven to earth and preserve her creation. Spider Woman saves her people yet again after the destruction of the Third World, when she opens a path through the dome of heaven and leads her people into the Fourth World, the present earth, providing hope and direction through an inner light that shines even in utter darkness.

When Spider Woman appears:

The more you reach for what inspires you, the more your purpose becomes apparent. Saving grace is at hand.

Act in alignment with your beliefs. Believe in what you want to be. Even without a clear sense of direction or a specific goal, doing small good things will illuminate your next steps.

This is not the time to tackle a large problem head on. Use subtlety, humility, and thoughtfulness in your approach. Sense the pattern that exists behind the scenes.

You are part of a network, a luminous, radiant web that connects every living being. Feel your connections to the ones you love and to your special places on the earth. See these connections shine with clear and flowing light, light that flows through and fills you. Invoke this web in your meditations to send healing lights and energies to those in need.

XVIII Moon — Arianrhod
Welsh Goddess of the Moon

In the realm of the soul, the Moon is your guide.

Arianrhod, whose name means Silver Wheel, is the Welsh Mother of the Night, goddess of the moon, the sky, and the stars. She is a shape-shifter who often appears as an owl of the night, the owl who sees in darkness, who sees at once ahead and behind, whose wings are soft and silent. She is a weaver upon her wheel, braiding and binding her magic into the manifestation of the world and the destiny of its creatures.

Arianrhod is a virgin unto herself, living alone or surrounded by enchanting, otherworldly women. She enjoys her sexual encounters with men, however, especially with mermen in the ocean. Like other Celtic goddesses, she is a singularity that embraces duality—she is the mother of two magical children, although the tale that survives of her birthing them by stepping over a wand is strange indeed. Her children are Dylan, a spirit of the sea, and Lleu Llaw, a solar hero who is raised and taught by her brother, the magician Gwydion.

Her Silver Wheel is the Wheel of Time, both of seasons and of reincarnation. It is also the Wheel of Night, of the zodiac that eternally circles the North Star. Arianrhod has a tower behind the veil of the Aurora Borealis called Caer Sidi, the Revolving Fortress. It is the Tower between the Worlds, the Tower of Initiation. The goddess carries the dead to Emania, "Moonland" in her people's tongue, in her ship named Oar Wheel. Once in her palace, she instructs the souls in the magic and wisdom of the Otherworld. In Emania they await their understanding of their fate. In the Tower they prepare for their next incarnation. In the Land of the Moon, souls find the meaning and purpose to human life. Arianrhod invites her people to come to the heart of the power that reveals their nature and their mystery.

When Arianrhod appears:

Wear silver and moonstones.

A reenactment of an old story is at hand. The archetypes may be manifesting in your life, or in something from your own past that haunts you. Look with your night eyes, your soul vision, for a significant reinterpretation.

The situation involves deep forces and feelings. Change comes over time. Maintain your intention and stay with the process. Let it unfold; let it manifest differently than you have planned. Look for meaning and guidance among the omens you receive along the way.

Attune yourself to your rhythms. Listening to the intimate and innate knowledge of your physical being brings celestial wisdom into embodiment.

Set your imagination free to journey through time and space and bring back stories of power and magic.

Get more sleep. Your brain needs time to rest, heal, process, and be at its best. Your mind needs to wash itself in dreams, even if the visions cannot be remembered upon waking. But try to remember.

XIX Sun—Sekhmet
Egyptian Eye of the Sun

Power burns. Power heals.

Sekhmet is the Lioness of the Sun, the Eye of Ra (also called Re), and the Egyptian goddess of destruction. Her name comes from the word *sekhem*, "to be mighty." On her head she wears the solar disk and the uraeus, the cobra, symbols of holy authority, of divinity, sovereignty, and power. She is the raw power of the sun, born from his anger and the fire of his eye. Pure and wild, she exults in her rampages. She loves violence and passion, the fire in the blood, the burning of the loins, and the raging of the heart. She is the untempered sun. She is death in the desert. She is divine vengeance, born to destroy humanity for their wicked ways.

Once in full fury, she cannot and will not be stopped, although the now-terrified gods plead with her. Ra regrets his spite. The sun god thinks to dye beer with ocher to resemble blood. Seven thousand vats of the red beer are set in the path of the goddess. Sekhmet mistakes the beer for blood, drinks it all down, becomes intoxicated, and turns to seeking joy instead. Some say she becomes the goddess Hathor after this, that the Celestial Cow, beloved lover, mother, and muse, is her sweet side, as Sekhmet is Hathor's dark side, the mother's righteous rage.

Because of her terrible power, Sekhmet inspires great efforts to placate her. Her people create a "litany in stone" for her. Over seven hundred statues are placed in harmonious, celestial alignment, and with daily rituals of appeasement, the goddess will never grow so angry and destructive again.

Yet, the Lioness is also called upon by healers, those named a "pure-priest of Sekhmet." Her cleansing fire protects against the devastations of pestilence and plague. Her amulets safeguard the wearer from premature death. Sekhmet ensures that the pure flame of one's life is not cut short before it burns all it can.

When Sekhmet appears:

The situation challenges you to exert your utmost power and influence. Be strong. Be mighty. Be unapologetic. Devour your fears. Do not let small things trouble you now. Juice up your life. Drink in the sweetness. Play in the sun. Give your one precious life all your blood, sweat, and tears. Letting your passions roar makes life beautiful and momentous.

Own your rage, your outrage. Out the evildoers. Stillness and silence do not protect you. Ferocity does, but take care not to punish the innocent on the way. Remember you have a sweet side.

Burn away the corruption that clings to your spirit by feeding your spirit what makes it whole and strong and on fire from within.

XX Liberation—Persephone
Greek Goddess of Resurrection

The past is not forgotten, yet life begins anew.

Persephone is the Greek goddess of life, death, and resurrection. She begins her immortal life as Kore (Maiden), a nymph of flowering meadows and daughter of the great goddess Demeter. She becomes the dread and powerful queen of the underworld. The story of her transformation is the basis of the Eleusinian Mysteries, the ancient teachings and rites that promise initiates a blessed afterlife.

Kore is lured away from her companions by the most beautiful flower she has ever seen. When she bends to touch it, the earth opens beneath her feet. Hades, god of the underworld, has been watching. He wants her for his wife and makes his move. From the chasm, Hades bursts out in his chariot drawn by black horses, and Kore is seized. Hades turns his chariot toward home, and the earth closes over their passing.

The nymph becomes his queen and sits by the side of the lord of the dead. She is the only one who may overrule his judgment, previously an absolute sentence to the punishment pits of Tartarus, the ghostly wanderings of the Asphodel Meadows, or the eternal bliss of Elysian Fields. She introduces the quality of mercy into the underworld. She becomes Persephone, She Who Shines in the Darkness, She Who Shines for All.

The goddess does not remain in the darkness below. Her mother, Demeter, has turned the world around to make the gods bring her home to the upper world. But Persephone has eaten the food of the dead, a few pomegranate seeds, and so she belongs to both worlds. Her journey gives the world the cycle of the seasons, and the understanding of the processes of growth, decay, and rebirth. For the initiates of the Mysteries, she provides not mere mercy but revelation and transcendence. Through the grace, the sacrifice, and the power of Persephone, they find release altogether from the eternity of the underworld. Like their goddess, the initiates break free of and transcend the cycle, and they look to join their souls to her forever.

When Persephone appears:

The situation is charged with meaning and potential. You have the opportunity to break a negative cycle, to break through to another level of awareness, and an opportunity to exercise that awareness for a great good.

Two worlds exist for you: the spiritual and the mundane, the real world and the Otherworld, the lands of the living and the dead. You are walking them both, so give each their due of thought, respect, and care. Two halves are less divisive the larger you become.

Pain and shock are not the end of the story and are not the definition of your life. Healing and power are. You have far to go. You have the resources to get there.

Follow a calling. Follow the dream. It is time to find your path from here to fulfillment.

XXI World — Coatlicue
Aztec Mother of Creation

A single manifestation holds a multitude of being.

Coatlicue, whose name means She of the Serpent Skirt, is the Aztec earth goddess and the Mother of Creation. She is the mother of the gods, the sun, the moon, and the stars. She creates life and she receives the dead. She is the full circle of initiation and completion. She is one and many, for Coatlicue has four sisters. She is a fivefold goddess; she is the fivefold earth with her four directions plus the center axis to make the whole. The earth is sunlit and moonlit; the earth is mother and murderer. The serpent, like the earth, has a dark side and a light side, as creature of the underworld and as bringer of wisdom.

Coatlicue's skirt of many snakes symbolizes her legendary fertility. She brings forth children as a virgin, either completely on her own or after touching feathers or jade stones or love charms delivered from the magicians of the sun to woo her. Her breasts are flabby and hang low from having nursed her hundreds of children.

The goddess is also the grieving mother who sees her children at war and mourns their death. And she is the devourer. Her face is skull-like, her hands and feet have claws for digging out graves, and she feeds on corpses. The earth gives birth to all that lives, consumes all that dies, and does both insatiably and perpetually. Behind Coatlicue is a representation of the Aztec calendar stone, showing cycles of time in the color of blood.

Coatlicue is feared because she brings darkness from the underworld to swallow up life. She is beloved because she is the flower-covered earth in spring. Her power is rooted, bountiful, and profound. Her aid is invoked to keep the teeming jungle at bay while at the same time encouraging crops to grow. She is abundant life, but life that comes with limits, life that comes with the recognition of death.

When Coatlicue appears:

You have done what you need to do and have been what you need be. Your life has come together in this moment to say that service has been enough. It is time to live according to your own rules. Take leadership of your life.

Invite Coatlicue's all-encompassing power into your day by adding cayenne, allspice, or chocolate to your morning coffee or tea.

Look for intelligence in overall design and longevity in performance when acquiring material objects.

If the situation were a multiple-choice question, the answer would be "All of the above." Your life is all these things. Since you have not yet exploded, you are more capable than you know. Realize that and get on with it.

Get creative in small, ordinary ways. Try a new food, wear a different color, hang a picture, make mud pies with children. Make time for something beautiful to happen in your world every single day.

The Minor Arcana

The suits of the Minor Arcana of the *Dark Goddess Tarot* are the four magical elements: Fire, Water, Air, and Earth. These correspond to Wands, Cups, Swords, and Pentacles but are more primal and more universal. Goddesses chosen for each suit have a connection to the element as well as to the traditional Tarot meaning.

The court cards represent areas of power of the Dark Goddess. For Independence, the Amazon. The Siren's power is her Sexuality. The Witch is a practitioner of Magic. The Hag walks with Death.

The goddesses of the suit of Fire are the Roman Vesta; the Greek Hekate, Circe, Eris, and Thyone; the Ainu Kamui Fuchi; the Celtic Epona; the Hindu Durga; the Tibetan Red Dakini; the Aztec Chantico; the Hawaiian Pele; the Egyptian Qadesh; the Welsh Cerridwen; and the Voudun Maman Brigitte.

The goddesses of the suit of Water are the Face of the Deep; the German Lorelei; the African Mami Wata; the Greek Lethe, Scylla, and Aphrodite; the Mexican La Llorona; the Egyptian Tefnut; the Irish Maeve; the Inuit Sedna; the British Lady of the Lake; the Mayan Ixchel; the Shinto Haya-Akitsu-Hime; and the Norse Ran.

The goddesses of the suit of Air are the Greek Nemesis, Athena, and Erinys; the Tibetan Blue Dakini; the Egyptian Nut; the Japanese Harionago; the Celtic Scathach; the Roman Laverna; the Hopi Crow Mother; the Irish Banshee; the Norse Skadi; the Babylonian Lilith; the Yoruba Oya; and the Hindu Dhumavati.

The goddesses of the suit of Earth are the Greek Gaia, Sphinx, Demeter, and Baubo; the Norse Hel and Norns; the Pacific Northwest Tsonokwa; the Sumerian Ereshkigal and Inanna; the Scottish Cailleach; the Nigerian Ala; and the Chinook She Who Watches.

Ace of Fire — Vesta
Roman Goddess of Holy Fire

Revere the source. Keep power pure.

Vesta, the Roman goddess of fire and the hearth, is a quiet, strong, and serious goddess. She dresses in modest robes of undyed wool and is shown standing in front of her temple, sacred fire and fuel in her hands. The fuel is gathered branches carefully bound together to create that which will burn longer than a haphazard pile of sticks. A virgin whole unto herself, when her brother Jupiter offers to give her anything she desires, Vesta asks to remain unmarried. She also asks for the first part of every sacrifice, to honor the spirit and power of the fire, the hearth, and all that has been made possible by gathering around it. Whether in a grand temple or a humble home, the first part of all oblations to the gods is given back to the fire herself. Good fortune follows when the offering crackles and speaks as it burns.

Unlike in the homes of the people, no image of Vesta is found in the temple, for there the fire is all, the goddess in her purest, most powerful form. The temple is circular in design, purposefully recalling the round hut of the primitive era, so that in its hearth the ever-burning fire represents the endurance of the heart of Rome; the holy fire is rescued from the fall of fabled, ancient Troy and is used to found a city whose fame would grow even greater.

Only on March 1st, the Roman New Year, is the fire allowed to go out before being ritually renewed. For the fire to be eternal and continue to protect the state of Rome from disaster, it must be kept burning, no easy task in a building with a vented roof. Assigned to protect and feed the fire are the Vestals, maidens chosen from noble families to serve the flame for the next thirty years of their lives. Their devotion and their chastity must be exemplary as they emulate Vesta's desire to blaze forever in purity, passion, and power.

When Vesta appears:

The situation in question has deep roots and a bright future. The grounding of the one and the inspiration of the other work together for success.

When what you want arises from your elemental spirit, let it find some expression. Acknowledge this desire or risk your spirit fading away. You need to feed your flame.

Do not allow critics or helpers to skew your vision, nor allow yourself to twist it to fit your fantasy or your convenience. If you are granted a true vision, honor it.

Begin a new daily practice that expresses gratitude for what makes you feel alive. The time is right for your choice in this practice to become quite meaningful.

You know what makes you stronger. Do that now.

Set aside a special place just for you to commune with your spirit. Clean and refurbish your altar with what is most meaningful.

Two of Fire — Hekate
Greek Goddess of the Crossroads

You don't need a path to find your way.

Hekate is a mystery goddess; a Titan, one of the old gods from before the Olympians came to the land of Greece. She may be the only one who survives the war between the gods with her powers intact. In Latin she is named *Hecate Trivia* (Latin for "Three Roads") because she retains her powers in the three realms: heaven, earth, and the underworld. She walks all roads and knows all ways. She is the goddess of the crossroads, for where roads cross, there is blood and power; there are ghosts and opportunity. In Greek she is called Phosphoros, the Light Bringer, and Nyktipolos, the Night Wanderer. She opens the passage; she illumines the path. Hekate is a psychopomp, a conductor of souls, one who can guide another between the worlds.

Hekate, along with Demeter and Persephone, is one of the goddesses of the Eleusinian Mysteries, ancient rites of life, death, and resurrection, of seasons of the land and cycles of the soul. When Demeter is frantically searching for her missing daughter, Hekate speaks up to let her know what has happened. Her flaming torches guide the mother through the night. When Persephone is released from the underworld, Hekate lights her way home. When Persephone returns to rule the land of the dead, Hekate goes as her minister and companion. The Eleusinian rites were practiced for 1,500 years and embraced thousands of souls, yet every initiate kept secret the ultimate revelation. Perhaps because revelation, like the night path, the soul's path, illuminates differently for everyone. Perhaps because mystery can only be experienced, not explained.

For some, Hekate's familiarity with the underworld has cast a shroud of fear upon the one who wanders dark ways accompanied by the hounds of Hades. Some name her Queen of Ghosts and Mother of Monsters. The wise know she is called Goddess of Witches because she walks their walk, the spirit's walk between the worlds.

When Hekate appears:

When next you hear a howling dog, think about the path you are on. Consider how you can take it to a more meaningful, more magical place.

When you are at a crossroads and have a choice to make, move toward what you know is true over what you wish were true. Success comes when both intuition and reason are respected and offer equal guidance.

Accept the next meaningful opportunity that appears. Trust that if you take the first step, you will be guided to the next.

Light two candles. Set them in front of you. Notice the space between them. Slowly move them apart and see the space between them open up. Do not focus your eyes but allow yourself to visualize the way ahead opening up before you.

You may wish for power, but if you are reluctant to step up and take it, to seize the moment, it will remain mere wishful thinking.

Three of Fire — Circe
Greek Goddess of Magic

Ideas have a life of their own.

Circe (usually pronounced as in Latin *SUR-see*; in Greek, *KIR-kee*) is an immortal *pharmakeia*, a sorceress, the goddess who is credited with the invention of magic. She lives on a sacred isle far from inhabited lands, located on the boundary between the sea and the river Oceanus, which encircles the earth. Friendly lions, bears, and wolves run through the halls of her home.

Circe knows the lore of every leaf, root, berry, and flower. She blends medicines. She mixes potions. She heals and she poisons. She creates illusions that please her, glamours that hide or reveal. She is a necromancer, raising the shades of the dead to discover hidden information or foretell the future. Circe is known to be a friend to witches; an ancient invocation asks her to "come cast cruel spells; hurt both these men and their handiwork."

But Circe's most famous skill is metamorphosis, the transformation of one body into another, as the men of the wanderer Odysseus discover when they chance upon her shores. She pours an elixir into their drink of honey, wine, barley, and cream. After they drink, she touches her wand to their hair and chants a spell: bristles sprout on their faces, their words become grunts, and they are changed into animals. After Circe makes peace (and makes love) with Odysseus, she unspells his men by similar means, returning them to themselves. She then advises Odysseus on the rest of his journey, foreseeing what he will encounter. Her advice allows him to survive the dangers. She is not jealous, knowing he will have other women before finally coming home to his wife. She has had her fun, and there are more potions to brew, more magic to cook up, and more powers to discover.

When Circe appears:

Your creative ability is high right now. Make the most of it and make something. Express your creativity in any and every way you can: through participation in the arts, or by planting or arranging flowers, inventing a recipe, or developing a personal style.

Permanence is an illusion. And permanence is boring. Everything changes. Everything dies. But the journey can be a good one, and a legacy of work, of service, of knowledge, and of creation can remain.

Mix up the things in your life. Do not keep everything in separate pigeonholes. Bringing in new elements adds vitality to the situation. But do so with thought and skill.

Changing the appearance of your self or your home is not a superficial act. It reverberates on other levels and creates deeper change. Dress for power and pleasure rather than conformity or invisibility.

Four of Fire — Kamui Fuchi
Ainu Goddess of the Hearth

Family, ancestors, and gods meet at the hearth.

Kamui Fuchi, whose full name means Rising Fire Sparks Woman, is the goddess of the hearth for the Ainu, the indigenous people of the islands north of Japan and east of Russia. The goddess appears as an Ainu woman with a beautiful lip tattoo and richly appliquéd robe. Kamui Fuchi lives within the four-sided hearth that is at the center of every Ainu home. Her hearth is a portal, a gateway through which people and kamui can communicate. Kamui are the gods, the immortal powers of land and nature. Kamui is also the word for a sacred animal, especially the bear, for that is the form the gods most often take when they visit the earth.

The hearth is also the home of the beloved dead. For Kamui Fuchi's people, the word "ancestor" translates as "one who dwells in the hearth." The souls of the dead who live within will be given new bodies in time but live for the moment in the pure grace and power of the home fire. For this reason, and to keep Kamui Fuchi's blessing upon one's home, the hearth must be purified with rites, kept clean and tended, and the fire must never be completely extinguished. To keep this channel open among the living, the beloved dead, and the gods is Kamui Fuchi's primary purpose and power. This is so important that she never leaves her home. But her power is so great that she never needs to leave. She has mighty magic that can work at a distance, plus friends among the household kamui, such as the god of the privy, who will do her bidding.

Being the center of the home, Kamui Fuchi is the judge of domestic affairs. She chastises those who do not maintain proper relationships within the family, and punishes those who pollute the sanctity of the hearth and disrespect the gods and ancestors.

When Kamui Fuchi appears:

Scry using fire to receive messages from gods or ancestors. A wood fire works best, but any flame may be used. Scrying involves a soft gaze and an open mind. Let the spirit ones speak as they will, whether in thought, image, or simple symbol.

Clean your house. Smudge your home and yourself with sage to purify the energies. If you are allergic to smoke, use an aromatic spray of a few drops of essential oil mixed with the water. White sage is traditional, but you can use any herb or scent you find clean and refreshing.

Every home needs a hearth, a heart, a center. Every heart and hearth needs tending. If the relationships within your home are fraught with stress, then relaxation and some simple care are in order. Gather your loved ones. Celebrate your existence and value your connection.

Your life has been given to you by your ancestors. Acknowledge the gift even if you cannot honor those who passed it along. Remember that the fire they gave you is now yours to carry forward.

Your fire, your spirit and energy, has to last you all your life. Do not waste it in pursuits unaligned with your nature and purposes. Do not pollute your future through poor behavior in the present.

Five of Fire — Eris
Greek Goddess of Chaos and Strife

Run from trouble, it comes back double.

Eris (pronounced *AIR-iss*), the Greek goddess of strife, lives to create chaos. She stirs up trouble everywhere she goes, whether it is an unexpected quarrel among friends, a crowd gone riot, or a full-scale conflict. She accompanies her brother Ares, the god of war, into battle, delighting in the horrific and senseless violence. Her thirst for blood is insatiable. Even after the war is over, she haunts the battlefield, stalking through the destruction and gloating in her accomplishments.

Because Eris is such unpleasant company, she is the only goddess not invited to the wedding of the sea goddess Thetis. Angry, she turns up anyway. Out of spite and wickedness, she tosses among the guests a golden apple inscribed "to the fairest." Hera, Aphrodite, and Athena all claim it, and their rivalry will trigger the events that lead to the Trojan War and the devastation of an ancient city and people. Ruining a single wedding may have been the better choice.

Aesop tells a somewhat contrary tale of another of Eris's enchanted apples, but contrariness is one of the qualities of the goddess. In going through a narrow pass, Herakles sees an apple on the ground and tries to smash it with his club. Every time he strikes the apple it grows, until it completely blocks his path. He is dumbfounded and cannot think how to proceed. Athena tells him this is Strife: leave it alone, and it stays small; fight it, and it grows big. The hero learns that striking out blindly and violently does no good.

The older, perhaps wiser, Hesiod says that Eris has two sides. One is awful and cruel, but the other is not. Her kinder side is no less energetic, but what she bestirs is action among the shiftless and aimless, and what she brings is change.

When Eris appears:

Do not borrow trouble. Imagining potential conflict scenarios floods your system with stress hormones. This makes you touchy and so makes trouble more likely.

If you fight fire with fire, a conflagration will be at hand. Denial of conflict or anger may smooth things over for a while, but it will then burst out with more force, damage, and danger. Make more peace for yourself in the future by acting now.

Rage cannot be reasoned with, but it may be deflected. Humor or energetic activity may help.

If you are fighting with yourself, nothing can be achieved. Determine which parts of yourself are clamoring because they need a hearing and which just want to stir up trouble.

Six of Fire — Epona
Celtic and Roman Goddess of Horses

Succeed on the strength of your alliances.

Epona (pronounced *ay-PONE-ah*), the Great Mare, is the goddess of the horse. Her motto refers to the Celtic people's alliance with the horse, a partnership that allows her people to successfully make their way across Europe to the Misty Isles, and to flourish wherever they find themselves. Horses add tremendous strength, maneuverability, and wealth to the tribe. They can be used for meat, milk, riding, and hauling. The Great Mare is the source of the fertility of the herd, and so Epona is also the source of the potency and prosperity of her people. As the goddess of plenty, she is often seen riding sidesaddle accompanied by her mares and foals, and carrying a basket of the common and wonderful apples that mean food and drink, sustenance and sweetness.

When Roman warriors arrive in Britain, they embrace Epona and build temples to her, so impressed are they by the horsemanship of the Celtic people. Epona's warriors are a true cavalry. They fight on horseback with spears and swords, man and animal as one, quite unlike other armies of the time that ride to battle but then dismount or remain in a chariot to fight. The horse is the Celt warrior's greatest ally in war, partner in wealth, and friend for life.

Epona provides for her people in death as she does in life, for she is also the Night Mare. Her image is carved into gravestones, a prayer that she and her spirit horse carry one's soul safely into the next world. Seers of the tribe receive the visions she brings back to the land of the living upon her return and upon their awakening. The Night Mare's gift may show a path of good fortune, or inform a treatment of illness, or warn of danger, whatever is needed to sustain and increase the herd and the people who care for them.

When Epona appears:

Hang a horseshoe over the door to invoke the blessing of the goddess upon your movements throughout the day.

Make as much progress with the task ahead as you can today, and then tomorrow, until it is done. Prepare to move on to better things by clearing the road ahead.

When people who care for you are available to help you, let them. Have a plan and ask for small but specific commitments. Sometimes it takes a herd. And a herd needs a strong, sensitive, balanced leader. Especially when the herd is not of docile sheep but swift, spirited horses.

Prosperity means different things to different people. Know what it means to you. Be unashamed about what is enough. Be honorable about what is enough.

When you are offered it, enjoy your moment in the sun. Accept the accolades, take in the blessings, and store that sunshine. Let it give you strength as you go forward.

Seven of Fire—Durga
Hindu Fierce Mother Goddess

Rise up or the demons win.

The fiercest and eldest manifestation of the Great Goddess, Durga incarnates on earth to fight demons when they have become too powerful and threaten the continued existence of humanity and the gods. The gods invoke her into manifestation through offering their combined powers. Each individual god does not have the power to conquer the demons, but when all come together, a shining pathway for the invincible goddess appears. In Sanskrit, the word "durga" means "beyond reach," a place that is inaccessible, invulnerable, a fort and a sanctuary.

The goddess succeeds in vanquishing the demon armies, for when she needs help, female warriors arise from her sighs, and the insatiable Kali springs from her knitted brow. The tiger that Durga rides represents her unlimited power. The goddess commands and directs the wildest and greatest strength. She wears a red skirt, and the color red symbolizes action. She manifests for this purpose, for action. She keeps busy destroying demons and does not stop until the world is made safe. She works to protect her people from misery. The evils she slays are the selfishness, ignorance, jealousy, prejudice, hatred, anger, and arrogance that plague humanity. She disappears when the demons are defeated, because she does not need accolades and has no ambition upon the world beyond her purpose. She is the Divine Mother ensuring that righteousness and compassion will continue to exist.

In her hands are gifts from the gods, her many weapons: mace, sword, club, spear, lariat, bow and arrow, and the conch. The variety of weapons shows that one weapon cannot destroy every kind of evil. Different weapons must be used for different fights. The conch does not slay, however, but makes the sound of the sacred Om, the sound of creation, the sound of the preeminence and ultimate victory of virtue.

The Devi Mahatmya ("Glory of the Goddess"), a religious text that dates from the fifth century, speaks of Durga thus: Good fortune of the virtuous, Ill fortune in the house of the evil, Intelligence in the minds of the learned, Faith in the hearts of the good.

When Durga appears:

Know which weapon to use for the fight. To do this, you must first know what weapons you have available to you. These may be tools, talents, skills, or allies.

Know your ground, your position, and make a stand. Defend your rights and the rights of others. Do not confuse rights with privileges, nor convenience with virtue.

Identify your personal demons. Demons can be so subtle, and your compliance so ingrained. Remember that fierce compassion begins with self-care. Fight the demons, not yourself.

Do not give up because something is hard. It will be accomplished if you keep trying.

Will and energy together accomplish great things. Will without energy turns rigid and inert. Energy without will becomes scattered and chaotic.

Dress your altar with red foods, cloths, flowers, and fruits. Include arrows and other metal items and a mirror. Use camphor and sandalwood in your aromatics.

Eight of Fire — Red Dakini
Tibetan Goddess of Energy and Fervor

Let the rush lead to a new awakening.

The Red Dakini is the Tibetan goddess of fire and blood, of energy and sexuality. She bursts into manifestation from the realm of spirit. She surges in to engage this world, and transmutes everything she touches back to spirit. The yogini dances and leaps between worlds, creating paths and gateways through her movement. *Dakini* has been translated as "Flying Woman" and "She Who Revels in the Freedom of Emptiness." She comes from the land of the dakinis, a place of spiritual women west of Tibet called Odiyana, "Vehicle of Flying." The flight of the dakinis is that of the shaman, of the spirit that ascends to heaven and descends to the underworld seeking healing and lost souls.

The soaring Red Dakini initiates change in a great energetic shift, taking life from one level to another. She carries messages of synchronicity and fate. She charges the seed to burst its shell and enter the wheel of life. She revivifies the dead. In her presence, one is set free from old patterns of being and feels flayed, raw, alive. The dross is burned away and the shining core of spirit is revealed by the fire that holds both terror and bliss.

The Red Dakini seduces people to follow impossible dreams. She uses her beauty and desirability to inspire the most-spiritual quests. She is the fire of the body and the passion of the spirit in one primal, powerful, heavenly, beautiful being. Within the individual, the energy of the Red Dakini floods the system. She burns through mental barriers and physical blocks. She allows pain and pleasure to be felt in full, to shake the roofs and the foundations of body and soul. She purifies and invigorates her people who call out to her, who are willing to embrace her, fortunate enough to be chosen by her, and brave enough to love her.

When the Red Dakini appears:

The energy of the situation has momentum and direction that are difficult to divert. Get out of the way or go for the ride.

Activate your everyday life. Rather than seek convenience, welcome opportunities to move and to do.

Whether standing or sitting, elongate your spine. Invite a feeling of freedom and strength into your body.

Burn Tibetan incense. Ring a brass bell. Invite the goddess into your life if you are ready for change.

Follow your desire. Follow it to its source. Take your heart on the journey, be present and alive. Do not set your heart on a specific outcome. Do not set your potential for happiness in the future. Feel the potential alive in this moment, within your next heartbeat.

Nine of Fire — Chantico
Aztec Goddess of the Hearth

What you possess is worth protecting.

Chantico is the Aztec goddess of fire. She is the fire of the hearth as well as the fire found within volcanoes. Her name means She Who Dwells in the House. She is the life, the power within. She is present for every sacred and mundane activity of the household. Chantico is power contained, and power protected. She is a goddess of wealth, for hers are the glowing gems found deep within the earth.

Her emblem is the boiling cauldron. Her fire is represented by red and yellow flowers. The white and orange jaguar tails billowing from the cauldron are the symbols of smoke and flame. The jaguar, the potent, elegant predator of the jungle, is the avatar of the sun on earth. Chantico as the goddess of the hearth allows a piece of the great passion and power of the sun to be kept within a home.

Chantico defends the home and all that is contained within it, for the goddess of precious things is quite protective of her possessions: her jewels and beautiful clothing and furnishings. The unpleasant things she visits upon any human or god who dares to touch her property are legendary. Often she assumes the form of a poisonous, fiery-red serpent to achieve retribution. Underlining her prickly nature, she wears a crown of cactus spikes on her head.

It is said she is turned into a dog by the god of food when she breaks a taboo by eating after a ritual. But Dog is just another face she wears, as the dog protects the home. Folk who must leave their homes and go into battle bank a fire in their hearth and pray to Chantico that they may return before the fire goes out. The treasure most worthy of protection is the life that burns within their own bodies.

When Chantico appears:

Focus on your internal energy level. If the fire of your spirit is low, block those things that drain it. Invite those things that feed it. If it is running too hot, make sure it stays under your control. If you explode, you may lose what you have worked to achieve.

Build a fire. Understand what a good fire needs: fuel, air, and containment. If you have no fireplace or fire pit, an iron pot may be used, preferably out of doors. Fire is built in layers. First is an easily flammable tinder, such as paper. Then comes kindling, then larger pieces of wood. The larger pieces must be close enough to catch and feed each other, but not so close that they smother each other.

Watch out for what you treasure. Be aware, and do not allow the greedy, the needy, or the envious to ruin your pleasure in your home and possessions. Build a protective energy field by walking around your home carrying a candle, or passing a candle in a circle around the precious object. Make witch bottles from old jars filled with pins, nails, and other sharp objects, and bury them at your property line or keep them by your front door.

Ten of Fire — Thyone
Greek Goddess of Divine Frenzy

How far would you go to meet god?

Thyone (pronounced *thigh-OH-knee*) is a mortal who becomes a goddess, the apotheosed mother of Dionysos, the wild, intoxicating god of wine and nature. She is the high priestess of the Dionysian rites, the Bacchic orgies. She leads the Maenads, the "frenzied ones," in their tumultuous rampage through the mountains as they worship, writhing and dancing to their clashing cymbals, haunting flutes, jangling tambourines, and pounding drums.

Deified as Thyone, which translates as "inspired frenzy," the goddess is born Semele, a mortal princess of Thebes, a kingdom in central Greece. Her beauty attracts the father god Zeus, and they begin an affair where he comes to her secretly in the dark of night. Whether she is tricked by Hera, queen of the gods and Zeus's jealous wife, or whether she decides on her own, Semele asks Zeus to prove his love, and the god swears he will. What she asks is that he come to her in his true form, as he comes to Hera, so she may know what it is to sleep with a god. Bound by his oath, he does so, and she is consumed by thunder and lightning.

Her immortal son Dionysos is recovered from her womb. Some say Zeus gives the babe to the nymphs of a sacred cave, others that he sews the infant into his own thigh until the child should come to term. Still others say Dionysos leaps from his mother's blasted body, shining brilliantly as a star. Upon reaching adulthood he descends to the underworld to fetch his mother, or perhaps Zeus gives her a new body that has been bathed in and can withstand the purifying fire. Either way, the woman who would love a god, who would know the truth of god, becomes the goddess Thyone and takes her place among the immortals.

When Thyone appears:

Use storax in your aromatics, an ancient incense associated with the goddess. Or mix your own volatile oils, combining a passion-heavy scent with another that is sharp and strong as a mountain storm.

You cannot stop what is happening, or prevent it from overwhelming you. The only way out is through in this situation. Keep going. Do not give up. The future holds change that sets you free.

To prevent stress from sickening you, sweat it out. Drink hot teas. Eat hot peppers. Go dancing, go running, or take a sauna.

Go all out. An energetic response offers the best route to success. Keep pushing. Reaching for more brings you more than you dreamed possible.

Amazon of Fire—Pele
Hawaiian Goddess of the Volcano

A passionate heart should not be made tame.

Pele is the Hawaiian goddess of fire and the volcano. Daughter of Haumea, the Earth Mother, and Wākea, the Sky Father, she is *akua kino lau*, a spirit of many bodies. Pele appears as a withered crone, who may ask for a cigarette and light it with a snap of her fingers. She appears as a hot-blooded young woman who dances on the rims of craters. The goddess is passionate and can be vengeful when her passion is not requited. She falls in love with handsome young men, seduces them until she is satisfied, then returns to her mountain. There she appears as her elemental self, as a river of red running lava, or as steam rising from cracked black rock, or as fountains of sparks against the sky.

Pele is possessive of every bit of her land, which is both her home and her self. Travelers who pocket stones in Hawaii and take them away are known to have bad luck until those pieces are returned to her. Her people honor and appease Pele with heartfelt offerings, casting into her fires sugar cane, hibiscus flowers, money, and their own cut hair. Branches of the native berry bush the *ōhelo*, with its sweet red and yellow berries, are also offered. Sacred to Pele as well is a hardy and versatile flowering evergreen, the *ōhiʻa lehua*, the first tree to populate a new lava field.

In her ancient homeland Pele causes a great conflagration by playing with underworld fires. When the gods, her relatives, chase her from that place, she comes to the tiny atolls that are Hawaii. Pele creates island after island from them, bringing a new home into being for herself through raw power, through passion and need, through great eruptions of fire and earth. Resting within Mount Kilauea on the Big Island, the goddess divines her next adventure.

When Pele appears:

Love whom you love, whether or not your love is returned. Powerful emotion can be released through art and action, in hard work and hard play, through movement, words, and color.

Want what you want. Do not hold back in declaring your desire. Not getting it is better for you than not acknowledging it.

Do not overthink the situation. Learn to trust the core of the fire inside you, your life force and its impulses toward growth and expression.

Be open to adventure. Let passion lead you to a new land and greater power.

Siren of Fire — Qadesh
Egyptian Goddess of Pleasure

All acts of love and pleasure are my rituals.

Originally from the Middle East, Qadesh (Qetesh, Qedeshet, Qudshu) is the goddess of nature, beauty, sexual pleasure, and sacred ecstasy. Her name is from the Semitic QDŠ, which means "holy," and her titles include "mistress of all the gods," "beloved," and "without equal." Her epithet of Lady of Heaven, as well as her connection to both love and war shown by her two husbands, links her to other great goddesses from the East such as Ishtar and Asherah.

Qadesh arrives in Egypt in the time of the New Kingdom, bringing one husband with her, the Syrian warrior god Reshep. She acquires her other husband in her new land, the ever-ready, ithyphallic Egyptian fertility god Min. The goddess and her consorts are celebrated and worshiped together, as a triad.

Qadesh holds lotus flowers in one hand and snakes in the other. These represent not only female and male genitalia but her gifts of deep healing. She appears nude, facing front, standing on a lion, and wearing the crescent moon, all Eastern attributes. In her new land she is given the jewelry, hairstyle, and sun disc worn by Hathor, the Egyptian goddess of love and joy. Qadesh's Eastern ferocity is softened by Hathor's gentle influence and the embrace of her new people. She still has her warrior god at hand, but like the lion she stands on, his power is in service to his lady. Pleasure, not bloodletting, is his priority.

The marriage of two cultures symbolized by this goddess is inclusive. No husband is excluded for the other. Qadesh is made sweeter by the embrace of her Egyptian god, but her raw passion and powerful sexuality remain. She has the power to bring new love and new life from afar. She makes beautiful the union of separate bodies and diverse souls.

When Qadesh appears:

Balance and beauty are achieved by including all that you love in your life. Let all that you love serve and sustain you. Do not sacrifice one love for another. Be large enough to embrace more.

Know what brings you pleasure, and experiment if you don't. Take charge of your own pleasure through doing it yourself or communicating honestly with your partner. Sex is healing when there is mutual respect with care for oneself and for the other.

However you feel about your body, celebrate that it can be capable of pleasure, whether it is a lover or the breeze that caresses your cheek. When you stretch or move, do so as luxuriously and sensually as you are able.

Explore what another culture has to offer. See its sights. Savor its scents and flavors. Enrich your world.

Witch of Fire — Cerridwen
Welsh Goddess of Transformation

Craft anew with the bones of the old.

Cerridwen (pronounced *CARE-id-wen*) is the goddess of wisdom, magic, and transformation for the people of the western mountains of the Misty Isle who call themselves the Cymri (Friends). "Welsh," a word meaning foreigner, is the name given them by their British neighbors. Cerridwen is the keeper of the cauldron of the underworld, the cauldron of knowledge, of inspiration, and of regeneration. Her cauldron is the vessel where magic is made, where raw power is held, contained, directed, formed, and used to step from one state of being into another. She is a shape-shifter and a walker between the worlds. She often appears in the form of a white sow. The sow is fecund and fearsome. Sows are intelligent, have large litters of fast-growing piglets, and will eat their young during terrible times. Cerridwen is the Mother of Life, the Crone of Death, and the Mystery of Rebirth.

Cerridwen lives on a magical isle and gives birth to two children of opposing natures—a daughter, Crearwy, who is fair and good, and a son, Afagddu, who is ugly and mean. The mother loves them both. To help her unfortunate son, she brews a potion to make her boy the most inspired, inventive, and wise of men. Since it must brew for a year and a day to reach its full potency, she enlists a young boy named Gwion to help keep the pot stirred.

One day she is out collecting more herbs when a few drops of the mixture splash onto the boy's finger and he pops it into his mouth. Suddenly he understands the languages of birds and beasts. He knows the secrets of the past and can foresee the future. Realizing how angry Cerridwen will be at him for tasting what was not meant for him, he runs away. Returning, Cerridwen gives chase. They transform themselves through a cycle of the seasons as they run: a hare and a greyhound, a fish and an otter, a bird and a hawk, finally as a grain of wheat and a hen, in which form she consumes him, then gives birth nine months later to the great poet Taliesin.

When Cerridwen appears:

You have rich experience, special knowledge, a unique viewpoint. Claim it. Use it. See what you can create given direction, care, and time. Who you can become is worth the effort.

Use an established framework, structure, or container to help your creation develop. This keeps your energy focused and supported and protects it from dissipation.

In a contentious situation, keep changing tactics until you find the approach that succeeds. Think of the wisdom of animals and their differing, always evolving ways of surviving and thriving in the world.

Being whole means using your full power, embracing both the light and the dark, and knowing life and death together are one great mystery, one cycle of time.

Hag of Fire—Maman Brigitte
Vodun Queen of the Cemetery

Dance with your ancestors. Raise the dead.

Maman Brigitte is the Vodou or Vodun queen of the cemetery. Mistress of the Ghede, the *lwa* or spirits of the underworld, she is married to Baron Samedi, the chief of these spirits. She is foul mouthed, sarcastic, and suggestive. Her favorite drink is rum laced with hot pepper; her favorite sacrifice is a gleaming black cockerel. She loves to dance. She loves to shock. And she passionately loves her children.

Maman Brigitte has the power to raise the dead. She aids and cures lost cases and causes, those on the brink of losing the flame of their lives through evil magic and bad luck. In one song to Maman Brigitte, her people exhort her to arise: "A lot of talk won't raise the dead. Tie up your head..." and get along with the punishment of the evildoers.

The grave of the first woman buried in any cemetery is sacred to the goddess, who is the mother of the ancestors and therefore the source of life and death. Her ceremonial cross can be erected at this grave, and offerings to Maman Brigitte left there. The consecrated grave provides a pathway for energies to cross from one world to another, for wisdom to be received from the ancestors, with love and hope offered to them.

On November 2, Fet Ghede, All Souls' Day, her people dress in white or in the Ghede's purple and black and visit the graveyards. They burn candles, make offerings, and pray to their Maman for protection, justice, and healing. Offerings include rum and cigarettes, peanuts and plantains, coffee and cornmeal. The ancestors must be fed if one would have their blessing. Cornmeal is used to outline her *veve*, the sacred symbol that draws and nourishes her, so it may be blown or swept away. Nothing should remain once the prayer is complete and one has put the problem into Maman Brigitte's hands.

When Maman Brigitte appears:

Honor the ancestors. They are both your past and your future, where you came from and where you are going. Respect the ancestors who created not only you but everything around you. Honor them through offerings: on the altar, at the cemetery, or in person, through a visit to family or the elderly.

Do something a grandmother or beloved elder liked to do. Remember what they taught you. Pass their wisdom along to someone else so it continues to be alive.

Visit a cemetery and look for the oldest stones. Be respectful. Do not chatter. Never walk across a grave, but walk softly at its foot. Listen to the spirits. Do what they ask if it is within your power.

If you would make a change in your world, if you ask for healing or justice, remember to "tie up your kidneys" (gird your loins, as another might say) and get on with doing all you can on your own behalf. The ancestors and their Maman join in when they see you are serious.

Ace of Water—Face of the Deep
Ancient Nameless Goddess of Water

The sea knows all souls.

The Face of the Deep is the ancient, nameless goddess of water. She is Water by no other name, Water in no human form, Water at her purest, her deepest, her most enveloping and embracing. Science describes water as the universal solvent, the one compound that dissolves almost everything, given time. Water is the solution that makes connection, absorption, reaction, and union possible.

In Sumeria, the Face of the Deep is Nammu, the goddess of the primeval sea. Nammu gives birth to heaven and earth and to the first gods of the world. It is also she who dreams the creation of humanity deep within her body mind, and she offers this vision, this reflection, to the gods to make manifest. In Babylonia, the sea goddess who is mother of the gods is called Tiamat. The Hebrew word for the Deep, *tehom*, derives from this ancient name.

Before the Hebrew god speaks his famous words, "Let there be light," She Who Is Water already exists. The King James Bible speaks of her thus: "And the earth was without form, and void; and darkness was upon the face of the deep. And the Spirit of God moved upon the face of the waters." The Face of the Deep is God's lover, and it is this movement, this connection with the source, that catalyzes his power and allows life on earth to begin.

Water is the Ancient Mother. She is the primordial sea, the great womb, the birthplace and the reservoir of life. She is the heart and soul of the world. And she is the world of the heart, with all its passion, compassion, and pain. The Face of the Deep is the source of one's soul, the gift and the repository of the longing to become One and All.

When the Face of the Deep appears:

Nothing is more important now than the understanding of your soul's desire through the experience of this emotion. Emotion is a pathway to a deeper understanding of meaning. Discover where this feeling is taking you.

Reach out as far and as long as you are able. Success comes from being inclusive.

There is depth within you beyond even profound pain and vast love, a place that is boundless and eternal. If you can reach it, this ancient source will fill you from your core to your tips. It can also appear as a huge emptiness within. Do not be afraid of that. It is your soul showing you what a great capacity you have for life.

Look for relief in salt baths and herbal elixirs from old recipes. Flood your system with all that is loving and healing. Pour warm tea down your throat. Pour sweet sounds into your ears. Let the barriers of disease dissolve in the comfort of communion.

Two of Water — Lorelei
German Spirit of Eternal Desire

The deeper you go, the harder your heart will beat.

Lorelei is a siren who sings in the stone of the cliffs along the Rhine River, luring German boatmen to join her in an eternal embrace. A maiden of most alluring beauty, she ends her human life by throwing herself into the river in despair over love and is transformed into the Song and Spirit of Desire.

Her despair and her betrayal are twofold, for the sailor who is her one true love is faithless, and he abandons her after the consummation of their desire. Lorelei is also betrayed by the many men of her village who desire her. She does not try to seduce them, but they cannot resist her loveliness. Because Lorelei is lonely, open hearted, and generous, she does not resist their advances, and she is the one blamed for the subsequent scandal and disgrace.

Accused of witchcraft, she is brought before the bishop. His severity breaks down under her beauty and sweet simplicity. But when he would set her free, she begs instead to die, for if love has forsaken her, if strife is all that comes to her in the name of love, she would rather not live such a life. The bishop instead rules that she enter a convent. Three knights are sent to accompany her there. When their path leads them past a high cliff overlooking the Rhine, Lorelei asks to have one last look. The knights cannot deny her. They tether the horses and the four of them climb to the top. At the edge of the precipice, Lorelei cries out, seeing her errant sailor lover on his boat in the river below. At her cry he looks up. His boat founders at the same moment as she leaps, and the lovers are finally and forever reunited in death.

When Lorelei appears:

Rationalizing your desire does not make it rational; do not try. Reason may speak to consequences of behavior, but not to why or where to love. Be honest with yourself, if with no one else, about what you deeply yearn for.

Allow yourself to yearn deeply. You are not avoiding pain by denying love, but making life colder. Death lies at the end of every road. Make the journey a passionate one, one worthy of song.

Beware of projecting your passion onto someone else. Own your desire. Putting responsibility for it onto another is another form of denial.

Your heart is the generator of your personal electromagnetic field. Feel how every beat increases the power of your aura, charisma, and magnetism, your power to attract your desire to you.

Open your heart to the variety of possible expressions of desire. Release expectation over the form in which love should appear. Reach for the essence of the other being with the essence of yours.

Three of Water — Mami Wata
Igbo Goddess of Ardor and Fidelity

Dance for yourself, for the tribe, for me.

Mami Wata is the Igbo goddess of water, and a goddess of both ardor and fidelity, lust and faithfulness. A goddess of such beauty that her name is a slang term for a gorgeous woman to this day. A goddess of such depth and allure, her worship has spread beyond Nigeria to both sides of the Atlantic. While not human, Mami Wata may appear so when she chooses. Her true self is a mermaid-like figure, the upper half of her body a woman and the lower half a fish or serpent. A large snake, the symbol of divinity and divination, sexuality and healing, is her favorite companion.

Mami Wata is both benevolent and dangerous. She abducts people when they are in or on the water, and carries them away. Should she allow them to leave her spirit realm, they return home wiser, growing wealthier and more attractive afterward. She offers rich gifts to her lovers but demands they be faithful to her in return. Refusal, or agreement with subsequent infidelity, guarantees to bring bad luck.

An incurable or recurring illness is seen as a sign that Mami Wata is taking an interest in a person. When this is the case, only she can cure the afflicted. Offerings she appreciates are special foods such as sugar and biscuits, liquors, perfumes and incense, jewelry and bells. Devotees of Mami Wata wear red and white clothing in honor of her dual nature. Red represents her destruction, heat, physicality, and power. White symbolizes her beauty, creativity, spirituality, and wealth.

The core of her worship is dance, rhythmic yet abandoned movement, to African guitar, drum, and flute. The dancer's passion is what Mami Wata desires most. Whether celebrating alone or together, her followers will dance until they go into a trance, opening their souls and giving themselves to the goddess, so she will speak to them and through them and bless their lives.

When Mami Wata appears:

Love your friends and lovers faithfully, with spirit, sincerity, and action. Celebrate their existence with presents and a party.

Rhythm is ebb and flow, the alternating of sound and silence over time. Use rhythm to understand the dynamic of your situation, and you will know when to pull back and when to push forward. When you need to pull back, rest your heart in quiet communion. When it is time to go forward, take the next step.

Listen for the rhythms within you. Center upon your breath. Try to feel your heartbeat. See if you can sense the echo of something deeper and more mysterious sounding in your soul.

Merge with music, anything from a simple rhythm to a symphony. Listen, dance, sway until you forget yourself, until you know yourself as ebb and flow, sound and silence, power and creativity.

Four of Water — Lethe
Greek Goddess of Forgetfulness

Let the memory of evil be washed away.

In human form, Lethe is a lithe and lovely maiden. In water form, she is the River of Oblivion. She is a nymph, a Greek nature goddess who inspirits and embodies a specific natural phenomenon. For Lethe, her place and her being is one of the sacred rivers of the underworld in the realm of Hades. She flows around the cave of Hypnos, the god of sleep, where her murmuring encourages somnolence among the restless and disoriented shades of the newly deceased. Some souls remain caught here in Hypnos, and they will sleepwalk through eternity.

Souls who are destined for reincarnation gather at Lethe's banks. They drink deeply of oblivion, of the "waters that quench man's troubles," as the Roman writer Virgil says. The memories of the dead must be washed away before their spirits may return to the world of the living. Whether the memories are created through joy or pain, old bonds twist a soul trying to grow a fresh new life. So all must be released, dissolved, and forgotten before regeneration can begin.

The shadow side of Lethe's draught is unmindfulness, forgetting without the intent of healing or renewal, the oblivion sought by the lazy or evasive. Her name means both forgetfulness or concealment. The Greek word for truth, *aletheia*, is that which is unforgotten and unconcealed.

There is another sacred water in Hades, a sister to Lethe, the goddess Mnemosyne, or Memory. Initiates of the mysteries know they may drink instead from this river when they die, if they believe they are wise enough to be as open and vulnerable as a child while maintaining the awareness of all they once were. The wise understand that assimilation with subsequent transformation contains its own form of release and freedom.

When Lethe appears:

When things feel empty and stale, do not worry and do not sulk. It is a sign of change. Give it time so you can see which stale things are truly dead and which can be revived. Work this process before starting something new. Do not hold on to what requires too much of your soul to take. The new life is waiting. This is how you get there.

In purposeful forgetting, painful memories are not made nonexistent, they are made nontroubling. When one arises, imagine putting it into a box, separating it from your immediate awareness. Do it until it stays in the box. Then take a nap. When you are ready, open the box and watch the memory as if it happened to someone else. As you watch, make it smaller. Make it not you anymore in there, until you can just stop watching.

Make sleep sacred to be better rested. If you must have noise to fall asleep, make it gentle music or the sound of waves, not talk or television. Wash your sheets and toss a washcloth scented with a few drops of lavender oil into the dryer with them. Drink water from a blue or lavender glass and ask Lethe to take away today so you can better face tomorrow.

Take time out from your current task. You need a break to be able to continue more intelligently and effectively.

Five of Water—La Llorona
Mexican Spirit of Grief and Remorse

Fresh tears today or bitter tomorrow.

La Llorona, the Weeping Woman, wanders the arroyos of the Sonoran Desert of northern Mexico and the southwestern United States. She arises from the water, crying for her lost children. Living children must not answer her calls, lest she drag them into the river to drown, eternally repeating her crime and her pain.

She is a mother who drowns her children to get revenge on her cheating husband. She is a mother who drowns her children when they get in the way of her desire for another man. She is a mother who neglects her children until they are murdered by wicked men and tossed into the river. She is a mother who neglects her children and lets them be killed by the dangerous rising waters. Her story varies but the horror is the same.

After her children are dead, La Llorona kills herself out of grief and pity and rage and spite. She cannot enter the afterlife until she finds her children and brings them with her. But her innocent children have moved on. They will never be found. La Llorona cannot see that; she cannot let go of her guilt. She cannot stop feeling the pain. She weeps and weeps. She sees only her tears. Still she is drawn to children, to the vulnerable child she can grab with her cold fingers, to one she can claim and cling to for a few brief moments until that little one is lost as well.

Some say La Llorona is not a desperate spirit but the shade of a more ancient power of the land and her people, the Aztec Earth Mother Coatlicue, who weeps on the eve of the Hernán Cortés invasion as she foresees the fall of an empire and so many of her children.

When La Llorona appears:

Do not agonize over decisions made in the past, even those made out of anger or fear. It is done and the past does not change, and you do not want to keep living there. The present holds the only potential for healing.

Making a mistake once or twice does not make you bad at something forever. In the same but more serious vein, do not take temporary pain as proof of an eternal burden.

Something you must endure on an everyday basis has terms that may be negotiated anew. Stay open to discovering a less painful path of perseverance.

Try a homeopathic remedy for what is ailing you. Try homeopathic magic. Cry in the shower and feel the stream of water as your tears. Cry and let your powerful tears break up and wash away pieces of the pain. Let loose the river of your tears.

Look at what you do to avoid dealing with pain. Understand what results from this behavior, both in the long and short terms.

Six of Water — Tefnut
Egyptian Goddess of Dew and Rain

Renewal starts with simple pleasures.

Tefnut is the Egyptian goddess of moisture, of the rare and precious dew and rain. She is not the powerful Nile flood but a more intimate wetness. She rules personal moisture; she is the goddess of spit, tears, and lubrication. She is a goddess of pleasure and sweetness. Due to the lack of dogma in ancient Egyptian religion, many are the stories of her origin, but all agree that Tefnut is the product of parthenogenesis from some form of bodily fluid, from the spit, tears, or semen of a god. With her consort Shu, god of the air, she initiates the sexual cycle of creation and is the mother of Nut, the sky, and Geb, the earth. Clear water pours from her womb when she is pleased. Her priests pray to be purified by her sacred flow and be blessed by her power.

Tefnut wears the body of a woman and the head of a lion. She is called the Eyes of Ra, both the left and the right for the moon and the sun. Upon her head she wears the solar disk connecting her to the power of the sun and the uraeus, the cobra who represents sovereignty and divinity. She carries the ankh for the breath of life and the scepter for power. Tefnut's scepter echoes the shape of the papyrus flowers, another symbol of life and fertility. Papyrus is used to make so much of what is useful for her people, from boats and sails to ropes and paper. Its use as a writing medium helps ancient lives speak today.

Like other leonine goddesses, Tefnut can display a wrathful aspect. When she is angry, she withdraws the moisture that brings pleasure, eases hardship, and keeps life sweet. Yet, more often she shows her people a tender face, and the beautiful results of the gentle application of great power.

When Tefnut appears:

Success comes from choosing love over power and gentleness over force.

Keep it simple. This shows authenticity, not lack of sophistication.

Enjoy all of life that you can see, smell, hear, taste, and touch. Seek simple, everyday pleasures, not convoluted ones. Immerse yourself in a new environment so you can spend time just sensing, just being.

To recall a memory, think not about the details but about who you were then, how it felt to be you. Do not look at your life from the outside in. Life always comes from the inside out.

On a piece of papyrus or other special paper, scribe a fortune for your future self. Discover that a similar blessing was left to you in your past.

Seven of Water — Maeve
Irish Goddess of Intoxication

Drink from the cup. Enter the gate to elsewhere.

Maeve or Mab is the Irish goddess of intoxication. Hers are the liquors, mushrooms, and herbs that produce altered states of consciousness. Normal barriers break down under her onslaught, to release surging passion, blurting truth, dreamy vision, or true transcendence. Her name means Drunken Woman, yet she is also a wild and powerful queen who runs faster than horses, steals cattle on a bet, and starts a war to one up her current consort. In battle, she incapacitates the armies of her enemies by merely appearing; they are laid waste by their desire for her. She holds the hearts of her warriors in her hands, and they are at her command.

In tales of Maeve as the queen of Ireland, she sleeps with many an Irish lord, some say as many as thirty in one night. The deeper reality is that she is the goddess of the land who must endorse any man who wishes to rule. At their coronations on the ancient hill of Tara, Irish kings drink flagons of mead to produce the intoxication necessary to encounter the ardent goddess face to face and thigh to thigh. Maeve is another word for mead, the honey wine of bees, the drink of women's magic and mysteries, symbolic of menstrual blood. The king's willingness to please Maeve and drink the mead he is offered ensures he will rule well, being versed in the mysteries of the goddess and the land.

As faith in goddesses and memory of warrior queens diminishes, Maeve or Mab becomes known in her lands as the fairy queen, losing her sacredness but not her enchantment. The word "mabled" (Mab-led) means to be led astray by the fairies, be intoxicated by their otherworldly beauty, and lost to common sense.

When Maeve appears:

Your imagination is the gateway to success in this situation. Think from a place where there are no boxes. Use this power you have to see things inside your mind that are not seen with eyes open. Visualize the situation and ask that the answer be revealed.

Give your fantasies free rein. Do not get bogged down in practical matters, such as how you get there. Just like sleeping dreams, fantasies most often show scenarios of wish fulfillment or frustration. Also as in night visions, something unexpected can pop out in a daydream, given you have relaxed enough to veer off from the usual scripts. The daydreams will give your mind a vacation; the surprises will give you deeper information and direction.

Communication from your deep self is more symbolic than literal. A single symbol can hold an important message. Do not be unappreciative because of its simplicity.

Do not be put off or distracted by emotions that erupt from the inner world. Persevere through to deeper understanding. Emotions can be how your subconscious gets you to pay attention to the message, but may not be the point of the message.

Eight of Water — Sedna
Inuit Goddess of the Ocean and the Underworld

Going deep is not easy. Let it be worthwhile.

Sedna is the Inuit goddess of the ocean. She is the mother of the animals of the sea and the queen of the underworld, she who holds multitudes, past and present, in her tangled hair. She reigns from the bottom of dark Arctic seas. She reigns in a place beyond final breath. A place she created by leaving her life behind her.

Her many legends begin differently, but they end the same. While out on the ocean with her father, Sedna falls into the freezing water. Her father hits or chops off her fingers to free his kayak from her grip, sacrificing and abandoning his daughter to save himself. She comes to her death through the betrayal of one she loved and trusted, one who had the responsibility to care for her.

Her amputated fingers become the seals, whales, and fish that bless the seas and are her new companions. In the Eight of Water, the creatures shown with Sedna are, from top to bottom, beluga whale, walrus, bowhead whale, North Arctic cod, bearded seal, harp seal, ringed seal (the mainstay of Inuit diet, especially in winter), and narwhal. In the depths, her mutilation is transformed. Dismemberment does not break her; it multiplies her. She pulls her new life together by using her passion and fury, her energy and will. Her anger stirs the sea to violence, to life-changing, life-charging tempests.

Wise hunters treat her with respect. An offering of fresh water is poured into the mouth of every seal they catch, to thank Sedna for allowing them to feed their families. Living in salt water, Sedna is assumed to be always thirsty. Shamans send their spirits swimming down to her to comb her long black hair and calm her rage. Then she releases the animals from the deep and allows her people to partake in the bounty of the sea.

When Sedna appears:

Care for the child who has been betrayed. Care for the one who feels alone. Comb her hair. Tuck her in. Tell her a story. Let her tell you one of hers. Do not patronize or pander to lost spirits, but care for them.

Look at how old wounds may be operating below the surface, using irritation, compulsion, and pain to get attention. Understand links between cause and behavior. Then let a change in behavior become a path to healing the deeper wound.

Take a magical bath. Include salts in the water or use a salt scrub. Scrub yourself with loofah or pumice or cloth to renew your skin and imagine fresh life rising to the surface. Then add a soothing oil to the bath or spread balm on your skin to be tender to your new skin. Let its fragrance be complex, creative, and energizing.

Surrender to the depths. Pay attention to life's many levels. Drop superficial distractions. Devote your life where you feel great power at work. Commitment helps you survive the storms.

Nine of Water — Lady of the Lake

British Goddess of the Quest

Make a wish, take a vow.

The Lady of the Lake is the British goddess of the quest. Akin to other magical water women such as Morgan le Fey and the Washer at the Ford, the Lady of the Lake appears throughout stories of the Grail and King Arthur. Her name may be Nimue, Viviane, or Igraine, and her bequests are legendary. To those who seek sincerely, ask bravely, and promise integrity, she grants tremendous boons.

The lakes of Britain are rich reservoirs of sweet water and abundant life. But they are also mysterious and tricky to navigate. The shoreline shifts, the mud sucks at one's feet, the mists rise, and the way home is lost. The way to the world of magic and spirit is revealed. The swans that grace her lakes are the Lady's emissaries and carry her messages between the worlds. They herald her presence and embody her gifts of beauty, devotion, and transformation.

For Arthur, the Lady of the Lake provides an initiation into leadership and maturity. She manifests the sacred sword from her depths, bringing into the world the talisman that enables the hero to understand his purpose and claim his destiny. In another tale, the Lady is also the fairy woman who raises a child to become the most mighty and spiritual of knights, Lancelot of the Lake. The lady of many names is queen of a watery otherworld, an eerie but miraculous land that lies beyond the veil of mist.

She is an enchantress and a spellbinder. She beguiles the great Merlin into teaching her his magic. With his famous foresight he knows she will someday use this power to trap him within a tree or cave, and yet he allows it to happen. The lure of the Lady of the Lake and the pleasure of her company are impossible to resist.

When the Lady of the Lake appears:

Make a wish. Toss a coin into a wishing well or fountain. At a natural body of water, toss a pebble, a flower, or a feather. Make it beautiful, for this is an offering to the Lady of the Lake in return for her magic. Make it strong, and wish with all your heart.

Take a vow. If you want one thing more than anything, bind yourself to it. Not to the outcome, but to the quest for it. Then you will know when the steps you take lead you closer or take you farther away.

Scry at a body of water or by gazing into a beautiful filled cup or bowl. Empty your thoughts. Watch the play of light and air on water. Meditate on clarity and reflection and find the deep wisdom you seek.

Go out on the water. If you cannot, go to the shore or look at photos and imagine yourself there. Sail, canoe, kayak, row, float. Take a journey on the water, away from the earth, at the threshold of the sky and the deep, and experience an everyday miracle. Feel the congruence, keep your balance, and ask for more.

Ten of Water—Ixchel
Mayan Goddess of the Moon

Birthings and endings come in a flood.

Ixchel is the powerful, beautiful Mayan goddess of the moon. She rules over magic, medicine, and midwifery. She is present at the throes of life, in its beginnings and at its ends. Ixchel carries a snake and a jug of water. The snake symbolizes the power of regeneration, how life can be renewed after a period of dormancy or pain. The snake is both a line and a circle, the journey of an individual life and the presence of the cycles of time. Her serpent also represents sexuality, its use in both magic and medicine, and its resultant fertility.

In the Dresden Codex, a pre-Columbian book from the Yucatán painted on fig tree bark, Ixchel is seen inverting her water jar, bringing about the Great Flood. This is the yearly deluge that signals the arrival of the rainy season, that washes away the old year and heralds the new. This is the flood that cleanses the world and destroys it in order to make way for rebirth. It is also the gushing waters of the womb. When the sac breaks, birth is initiated and new life is imminent. Shown caught in her flood are ten faces from Mayan life: the monkey, the anteater, the kinkajou, the priest, the bat, the quetzal, the warrior, the dragon, the dead, and the jaguarundi.

Her beauty as well as her skill in weaving causes unending jealousy among the men in her life. Her controlling grandfather kills her with lightning bolts because she leaves him for a lover, but hundreds of dragonflies gather to hover and sing over her body for many days, until suddenly she springs up whole once more. Her onetime lover, the sun, is so jealous that she makes herself invisible when he comes near. She leaves him too, to follow her own path through the sky. When she is not riding the night, Ixchel spends her time nursing the women of earth through their pregnancies and labors into their new and larger lives to come.

When Ixchel appears:

Yes, it is all happening at once. Success is found in riding the wave, not in stemming the flow or sinking below.

The situation has a cycle and a timing all its own. Tuning in to it will make the process less difficult.

Surging emotions can leave you elated, drained, and nervous. Be aware of this uneasy effect before making decisions that need a clear head, but do not ignore the direction indicated by the power of those emotions. The clear head must allow itself to be balanced by the renewal offered by the surging soul.

Live your best life now. Rid your life of all the deadweight you can. Make room for new pleasures and passions. Give new energy to those things you must keep, and see how they can be reinvigorated.

Consider a pilgrimage to Ixchel's island of Cozumel or another sacred isle. The seas are rising. Do not leave it too late.

Amazon of Water—Scylla
Greek Monster Maiden

Don't let the fears of others drag you down.

Scylla (pronounced *skulla*) is a Greek sea dragon with the upper body of a woman, the tail of a fish or serpent, and six dog forelegs sprouting from her waist, of whom the ancient poet Homer wrote, "No one could see her and still be happy, not even a god if he went that way." The monster maiden haunts the rocks and caves of a narrow strait opposite the whirlpool daemon Charybdis. Ships attempting to pass through the strait to reach the Island of the Sun can expect to lose at least six men to her grasping paws, yet if they sail too close to the whirlpool the entire ship may be lost. To be "between Scylla and Charybdis" means to be caught between two equally unpleasant alternatives.

Some poets say Scylla is born monstrous. Others claim she is born a divine and lovely maiden who plays among the other immortal nymphs of the sea but becomes transformed into a hideous creature, punished for her beauty by a jealous goddess: the witch goddess Circe, angry at losing the attention of her current beloved, a sea god infatuated with Scylla. Circe tosses her magic herbs into the ocean pool where the nymph bathes to affect the metamorphosis.

But some say Scylla, like the once maidenly Charybdis, who three times a day swallows the waters of the sea and three times throws them up again, is punished for having a mighty hunger, for having a desire of her own. She is killed for stealing cattle for her dinner, the cattle of a god enraged over the loss of his wealth and fearful of the loss of his power. Blasted by a god but immortal, she rises again in a new and terrible form. This time, no one is going to mess with her. She will eat and love and destroy as she pleases.

When Scylla appears:

Make firm your boundaries. Learn to say no. Do not care so much about others that you lose yourself.

Steer clear of people who project their own motives onto you. Do not be deluded by another's delusion. Hold on to the reality of your feelings and your experience.

Being yourself means accepting yourself, warts and all. Never apologize for who you are, even when you have consequences for your behavior. Change the behavior but understand and forgive yourself.

How others feel about you does not define you and must not oppress you. But do not ignore the emotions of others in your social environment. Tune in. Forewarned is forearmed, and if someone is serious about hurting you, you need to know of it.

Strengthen yourself and purify your land by picking up trash around your nearest body of water.

Siren of Water—Aphrodite
Greek Goddess of Beauty and Love

Love is a risk you must take.

Aphrodite (pronounced afro-DYE-tee) is the Greek goddess of love and beauty. She comes from blood and lust. As the old god of heaven, Uranus, is castrated by his children, the Titans, his final ejaculation spurts into the sea, and Aphrodite arises from this fertile spray. She is called Foam Born and She Who Rises from the Waves. She rides on a great shell, heralded by passionate and playful dolphins. Seawater that drips from her hair becomes pearls. She alights on the island of Cyprus and is greeted by the Horae, lovely nymphs of nature, time, and the seasons. They clothe her in garments made of scented flowers: crocus, hyacinth, violet, lily, and rose. The goddess inspires and creates beauty all around her.

Aphrodite comes to Greece from the East. She shows her relation to the powerful sexual goddesses of ancient Mesopotamia most keenly through the stories of her mortal lovers, such as her beloved Adonis, the beautiful youth who becomes the god who lives, loves, and dies for the immortal goddess. And whom she causes to live again, albeit transformed.

When Aphrodite walks the land, all animals rejoice. As Homer writes, her mere presence puts "desire in their breasts, so that they all mated, two together, about the shadowy coombes." She is called "lover of smiles" and delights in odd pairings and in seeing passion overcome the haughty. The goddess herself chooses lovers from among divine and human males unreservedly and unashamedly. She engenders the desire for love, connection, and communion, whether that love be lusciously carnal, as the earthy Aphrodite Porne, or deeply spiritual, as the heavenly Aphrodite Urania. For the goddess, both sides are sacred; both forms are holy. She is all that enchants the spirit and arouses the body. And by so doing, she opens the heart.

When Aphrodite appears:

Use oils of Aphrodite's favorite flowers (or your own) as aromatics. Use the flowers themselves both as offerings to the goddess and as invocations of her beauty.

Being attractive and charming leads to success. Natural beauty or natural warmth makes it easy, but charisma can be developed. Use the mirror, one of Aphrodite's magical tools. Look at the expressions of your face. Look at the gestures and stance of your body. Look at your clothing and grooming. See yourself clearly, but in the best light and with the best of intentions. See yourself with the eyes of love. See what you would like to change, what is possible. Try it out, then get it done.

Use mirror magic to see the face of your future love. Stand facing a mirror in a darkened room. Look at yourself and say "Aphrodite" five times. Close your eyes, then repeat her name five times more. Open your eyes and look for someone to appear over your left shoulder.

Admit your desire. Constrain it if you will, but do not deny its existence. Decide how you can express it in a safe and honorable fashion.

Creativity combines your essence with passion and beauty and allows you to participate in enchantment. Do or make or find something you love.

Witch of Water — Haya-Akitsu-Hime
Shinto Goddess of the Sea

Every stream ends in the sea, there to rise anew.

Haya-Akitsu-Hime, also Haya-Akitsu-Hime-No-Kami, is the Shinto goddess of the sea. Shinto (the Way of the Gods) is the ancient indigenous religion of the Japanese people and is in practice to this day. The great power and blessing of the goddess is her eating of all the sins that are cast into the sea, the salt water able to absorb, dissolve, and cleanse the evil. Her people believe that the ocean is so broad and so deep, she can swallow any pollution and impurity that can contaminate mere human beings. In Shinto belief, humans are fundamentally good, and sin and evil are caused by evil spirits. Only Haya-Akitsu-Hime, the great ocean, is powerful enough to take in those spirits and take them back to their original existences, transforming them into pure energy.

Shinto is a faith offering its people direct contact with Kami (deity or deities). Regular worship and attendance at ceremonies and festivals are important to the well-being of the relationship between people and Kami. The purpose of most Shinto ritual is to keep away evil spirits through offerings and prayers. Purification rites are crucial before one may approach any enshrined Kami. Before the commencement of every great festival, a priest purifies himself by rinsing with water his hands, his mouth, then again his hands. It is a simplified, symbolic expression of full-body immersion and surrender to the sea.

The salt found in the sea holds the purification and protection magic of Haya-Akitsu-Hime. Salt is thrown before a sumo match in order to remove any evil within the sumo ground. In the entrance of a Japanese restaurant, a small mound of salt represents the cleanliness of the establishment. But it is the water of the encompassing, surrounding sea that holds her full powers of transformation, renewal, and transmutation of energy.

When Haya-Akitsu-Hime appears:

Demonstrate your ethics and your beliefs on a regular basis to walk the blessed way.

Look beyond the form into the essence of the thing. That is where power lies. When forms dissolve, all becomes energy. And energy can be reshaped and used anew.

Purify yourself in salt water, whether in the sea or in a tub. Immerse yourself as fully as possible. As you surrender to the power of the water, feel any anger, fear, shame, and grief you carry within you begin to melt away.

To separate yourself from a wicked influence, write or draw yourself and the evil spirit next to one another on the same piece of paper. Cut or tear the paper into two pieces, one showing you and one showing the other. Tuck the paper of yourself away in a safe place. The piece of paper showing the harmful influence is to be torn into tiny bits and flushed down the toilet.

In Shinto, making sounds such as clapping is a traditional way to communicate with Kami. Repetition of bowing and clapping is an expression of reverence and sincerity.

Hag of Water—Ran
Norse Goddess of the Drowned

Surrender to the sea to find her secret places.

Ran (pronounced *rawn*) is the Norse goddess of the ocean and goddess of the drowned. She lives at the bottom of the sea with her husband, the god Aegir, and their nine daughters, the nine maidens of the waves. The fishes and beasts of the sea are her flocks and herds. The Vikings love and fear the sea in equal measure, for the ocean brings them riches, power, and glory, but also death, suffering, and destruction.

The sea is called Ran's Road. During great storms, the road soars all the way to the moon and may lead a ship on a most uncanny journey, perhaps miraculous, almost certainly one way. Ran is called cruel, greedy, and insatiable, for the open sea is unpredictable and difficult to navigate. Knowing her moods can save one's life. When Ran becomes lonely or angry, she surges to the surface, stirs up a tempest, and reaches out with cold fingers for new humans to keep her company. She drags ships beneath the waves or shatters them against hidden rocks. She casts her net and gleefully collects the corpses. Whether people drown by her doing or not, she gathers them in.

On troubled waters, sailors tie gold pieces into their clothes as payment for her hospitality should they be washed away into Ran's world, for she can be welcoming to those who come to her hall beneath the sea, especially if they come with offerings of gold. Her daughters serve the assembled spirits food and their home-brewed mead, which is as fine as what may be found in Valhalla. When the ghost of someone who has been lost at sea appears at the funeral feast, the friends and relations know that Ran has received the wayward soul and given them a home beneath the waves.

When Ran appears:

Stop fighting an inexorable tide. Position yourself to take advantage of the movement as best you can, and go with it as you must.

There is something going on below the surface, something big that will change everything. Watch for the signs of a sea change.

Offer "gold" to appease the restlessness of the sea. Throw back the sand dollars and shells you find on the beach. Toss coins into a wishing well, imagining that the well reaches into the sea's depths. Make a precious offering to your own mysterious and unknowable depths, that they may bring you more gifts of joy than dismay.

Deep in your soul, you know where you belong, and where you do not. If you do not act on this knowledge, do not expect relief from your difficulties.

Your authority comes from your difficult experiences. Embrace it. Exercise it.

Ace of Air — Nemesis
Greek Goddess of Judgment

The first step in discernment: perceive what exists.

Nemesis is the Greek goddess of indignation, retribution, and judgment. A daughter of Nyx, goddess of the night, her name means Dispenser of Dues. The sword is her tool and her emblem. While her sister Tyche, the goddess of fortune, bestows favors indiscriminately and extravagantly, Nemesis is more discerning and perceptive. She witnesses the unjust act. She sees through the attempt to hide it. She sees past the pretty face. She points out who truly deserves reward and who does not.

The goddess grants the knowledge of what is right and good. She can advise on what is appropriate in any situation. Yet, because she is a check upon fortune, she is more often seen as the punishing power of fate. Nemesis meddles in human affairs in order to restore the correct proportions according to natural and divine law. She is a fulcrum; she senses when the equilibrium has been disrupted. She sees the result; she understands the cause. She brings loss to those who are blessed with fortune but are not humble, and suffering to those who are blessed with gifts but disdain them. In some stories of the Trojan War, Nemesis appears as the mother of Helen. She points an accusing finger at the couple during the young wife's seduction by the visiting Paris. She knows that no good will come of this disrespect to the human law of marriage and the divine law of hospitality.

She is nicknamed Inescapable; she is called the Executioner of Braggarts. She is invoked out of people's righteous indignation. She is called upon for divine vengeance. Even the gods can grow envious of excessive human happiness, as well as angry at humanity's thoughtlessness and inordinate pride.

Nemesis enforces the limits beyond which one should not proceed, lest one offend a power in this world or abase another human being as a result. She represents a fine and sharp morality. She is honor. She is conscience.

When Nemesis appears:

Paraphrase an old Greek proverb and state, "May Nemesis walk at my feet." Then, as long as your plan is a fair one, proceed boldly on your path, knowing that the goddess will deal swiftly and justly with those who cross you with malicious intent.

Something about your situation needs to be seen through. Apply objectivity to achieve clarity. Whatever comes up in your mind as a "But . . ." is exactly what needs examining with a dispassionate eye.

Mediate your ego. Much of what people believe they deserve, they do not. Some things are not a matter of deserving but of privilege and possibility. Stay humble.

Moderate your sacrifice. Nemesis is no more fond of martyrs than she is of narcissists.

Keep your promises. Let your word be more than just words. Let it be what you are known for.

Two of Air — Athena
Greek Goddess of Wisdom and War

Delay action only for good reason.

Athena is the Greek goddess of wisdom and war, guardian of the city of Athens. She stands on a pinnacle with her spear in one hand and her owl in the other. War and wisdom may seem contradictory, but the goddess does not delight in bloodshed. Her concern is the protection and welfare of her people, and when she engages in warfare, it is for the advantages the state can gain. She favors heroes who are distinguished for their cleverness and counsel as well as for their valor. The people of Athens choose the goddess and her gift of the olive tree over Poseidon's offering of the horse, opting for the peace and prosperity the wise one brings.

Athena is the daughter of Zeus and Metis, the most powerful god and the most wise of goddesses, and both qualities are found in her. She is called bright eyed, gray eyed, and fierce or flashing eyed. She discerns clearly, she decides justly, and then she acts with strength. Her wisdom and her power are dedicated to the service of her nation. She maintains the rule of law, overseeing the courts and assemblies. She is endlessly inventive, and her useful creations include numbers, weaving, the plow, the flute, the chariot, and navigation, inventions that are not made by accident but through thought and reflection. Under her care is all that provides prosperity and protection to the state, from agriculture to fortresses and harbors.

Homer calls Athena "unbending of heart" and "pure virgin" as well as "savior of cities." The goddess remains untouched by passionate love. She punishes any attempt upon her chastity and all interference with her sense of order and responsibility. A hymn of Orpheus speaks of her thus: "Mother of arts, impetuous; understood as fury by the bad, but wisdom by the good."

When Athena appears:

Give the matter a second thought. Impulsive action does not serve the greater good. However, do not get caught up with rethinking. When the same thoughts reach the same conclusions again and again, it is time for action.

The most-successful ventures have a good plan at their foundation.

Get your affairs in order. Be honest, direct, and straightforward in your dealings with others. Fight injustice through legal means. The situation is best served by working within the established system.

Do not allow desire to cloud your vision with what you wish to see. Instead, see what achieves results, whether the results you seek are within human society or a human mind.

Pray to Athena in words of wit and rhythm to receive her blessing.

Three of Air — Blue Dakini
Tibetan Goddess of the Knife

If it is not real and true, sever the ties.

A dakini is a goddess, spirit, or energy who makes herself manifest to participate in the world. In Tibet, *dakini* translates to "She Who Crosses the Sky" or "She Who Moves through Space." Blue is the color of the sky, of Shunyata, the emptiness, the absence of matter, pure potential, the source of all possibility and manifestation. The Blue Dakini heralds a vast awakening. She dances in emptiness, in the void. Her presence creates awareness. She describes the space of becoming. Her movement makes it possible for thoughts and ideas to emerge within the mind. Her dance creates paths through the depths of infinity. She is the messenger of heaven.

The goddess is also known as the wrathful dakini for her violence and ferocity. She stands on a prostrated human figure. She wears ornaments of bone and carries a hooked knife. She slashes the demons of ego and neurosis. She purifies the seeker by plunging her knife into one's chest, then cutting out and eating one's heart. Hers is not a gentle initiation. The Blue Dakini heals through destruction. She keeps the soul from bondage to desire, attachment, or obsession by removing the unmindful, uninitiated heart. She brings piercing pain but lasting freedom.

The ones who face her knives without flinching are given a white conch shell to replace their ignorant hearts. The conch shell when blown echoes the sound that creates the universe, the sacred Om, which will sound forever in the souls of those blessed by the Blue Dakini. The wisdom of the dakini is one of the Buddhist's Three Roots, or inner sources of refuge. When accepted, her power of destruction allows one to quickly cut through obstacles along the path. Ultimately, it serves to annihilate all form so only the true essence remains.

When the Blue Dakini appears:

Prevarication and false hope kill your soul by excruciating degrees. Face the harsh truth. Accept the pain so you can learn how it may be healed. Cut the lies out of your life.

Put something in the place of your wound, something that feels a step closer to goodness and wholeness.

Alternatively, open yourself to the emptiness. Expand into formlessness to sense a new and exciting potential.

Be all encompassing rather than specific. Specifics distract. Pare them away in order to get the bigger picture.

Four of Air — Nut
Egyptian Goddess of the Night Sky

Until the dawn, rest as a star in my body.

Nut (pronounced *noot*) is the Egyptian goddess of the night sky, the goddess of heaven, and she who holds you while you sleep. Every evening she reveals her glory. At the end of each day, she swallows the sun. The sun makes the journey every night that the soul does after death, traveling through the body of the all-embracing goddess of night. At dawn Nut gives birth to the sun again.

She Who Holds a Thousand Souls arches her naked body covered with stars over the earth. Geb, god of the earth, is her beloved. Lord Ra stops their embrace and separates them out of jealousy, and for fear that life cannot flourish should there not be some space between their bodies. Yet, the lovers rejoin during the five extra days of the Egyptian calendar, the five extra days Nut made from moonlight after winning the light from Konshu, god of the moon, in a game of chance. These days are time out of time, when the ruler of the world cannot touch them with his decrees and all on earth celebrate their freedom to love as they will.

Called Protector of the Dead, Nut is painted on the inside lid of the sarcophagus or on the vault of tombs, so she may enfold the soul placed within. Within the star-filled sky, souls are protected from all evil while they are refreshed. The dying pray, "O my Mother Nut, stretch Yourself over me, that I may be placed among the imperishable stars that are in You, and that I may not die." For a soul may die if it is eaten by the monster of the underworld at Maat's judgment. Nut, beautiful, all-embracing Heaven, provides for the possibility of mercy and grace.

The sky goddess, in arching her body above the earth, also protects all life, for it is she who creates the barrier that holds back the forces of chaos from destroying the precious order and peace of the world.

When Nut appears:

Give yourself some time to sleep on it before making a big decision. Get the information you need, then let your thoughts about it settle into place. Then it will be easier and more powerful when you do act or speak.

Dream or not, sleep or not, but go to bed. You need rest more than you need to be doing something else right now. You need a time-out from the struggle. Your body and your mind are refreshed through downtime.

If you are called upon to help others in illness or grief, do so from a place of gentle but lofty compassion that keeps your own heart whole and gives them the support and space they need to find their own way through the darkness.

Reconnect with those people, places, and things that bring you peace. Reduce the forces of chaos in your life by tidying your environment or listing your thoughts.

Five of Air—Harionago

Japanese Spirit of Mischief and Mayhem

The situation is without honor. Engage at your peril.

Harionago, also called Waraionago (Laughing Girl), is a Japanese spirit of mischief and mayhem, a ghoul with a deceptively lovely face. Her name means Barbed Maiden or Hooked Hair Woman. She is a demon, an immortal spirit bent on wicked and selfish ends, who takes the form of an enticing woman with long, beautiful hair, hair with its ends tipped in razor-sharp hooks. She uses her appearance and her marvelous hair to ensnare and prey upon trespassing young men.

In the night on a dark, lonely road on the island of Shikoku, Harionago appears, her luxurious, wicked hair piled safely atop her head. She will smile at a boy, tease and laugh at him, inviting him with her eyes to laugh back. If he does, if he dares, she loosens and unleashes her hair and attacks him with it. Her hair reaches out and grabs her victim, wrapping him up in its wiry power, its barbs mutilating him in the process. There is no purpose or reason in her action other than her pleasure in his confusion and pain.

One young man from the village of Yamada escapes after encountering her by running as fast as he can once he sees her hair moving. He runs to his house and shuts the door between them. At dawn, he opens the door to find the deep gashes left in the wood by Harionago's hair. Because it was a wooden and not a paper door, he escaped with his life, providing a moral tale about the importance of not wandering far from home after sunset, and having a good, solid home to run to, as well as a reminder to close the main door for the night, not just the inner door, against the evils that lurk in the dark.

A wise man avoids engagement with a spirit such as Harionago and respectfully and quietly withdraws as he is able, or does not walk those lonely dark roads. But youth is irrepressible and the demon is so cleverly alluring, so strangely challenging, that almost no one can be wise.

When Harionago appears:

If you would lose too much and engagement cannot be avoided, use your own cunning as necessary to extricate yourself. For now, you win by getting away.

The situation may not be lose-lose, but it is definitely not a win-win. A redefinition of the ground rules is needed before parity can be achieved.

Be wary. Someone is not being honest or may be incapable of honesty, given the situation. Look to yourself and not to the ethics of another to preserve your interests and integrity. During delicate negotiations, do not reveal your hand.

Do not bristle at every offense. Having a chip on your shoulder makes you a target. Leaving a chip on your shoulder builds a burden you must bear.

Six of Air — Scathach
Celtic Goddess of the Sacred Isle

Accept guidance and find your purpose.

Scathach (pronounced *SCAU-ahch*), sometimes called Scota, is the Irish and Scottish goddess of the arts of battle, healing, and magic. The great warrior goddess's name means She Who Strikes Fear. She is known as the Shadowy One and the Dark Goddess, and she lives on a distant and mysterious isle. She welcomes to her land only those who make an effort to get there. On her helm are the wings of a goose, the symbol of a Celtic warrior, as the goose is both alert and aggressive, making it an excellent guardian.

Youths journey across the water hoping to be taught by the dread and beautiful goddess, to be initiated by her into the skills of arms, the strategies of battle, the art of love, and the craft of magic. They come to stay for a year and a day and hope to be made heroes, perhaps to return with the special gift of an enchanted sword or spear. Scathach's powers include prophecy, and she may read their palm and foretell their future. After the students complete their courses, the goddess sends them back to their people to do great deeds.

Scathach also roams battlefields, collecting the souls of her heroes to guide them in their journey to the otherworld, to Tir Nan Og, the Land of Youth, the joyful ever-after. The goddess is generous with other souls on the Soul's Road, the Imrama upon which so many seekers of the Land of Youth may be lost, and will also help those not especially chosen. She will not lead the living, though, who out of curiosity or despair attempt the journey before their time. She demands they first perform the deeds they are meant to accomplish in their lives, and will offer the skills they need to do so.

When Scathach appears:

Prepare for the challenges ahead. If you do not have a sense about what they are, keep strengthening your position in the ways that you know work until the path ahead becomes clear.

Take the time it takes to learn something or to get somewhere. A leapfrog over the process does not succeed. Patience allows you to integrate key concepts and notice details you may otherwise overlook.

Learn from trusted teachers. Check out their history and their values. Align with those who encourage you to become a bigger person with a larger life.

Balance your mental and your physical activities. The best practices feed off each other to bring you to a place of integrated strength.

Take time out of your normal routine to make a spiritual journey, whether you have an hour or a week. Go see a rock, a river, a grove, or a guru. Restore your faith in yourself.

Walk a labyrinth. Leave your concern in the center. Allow inspiration or solution to be revealed on your return path.

Seven of Air—Laverna
Roman Goddess of Thieves

Cunning succeeds where clout does not.

Laverna is the Roman goddess of thieves, rascals, cheats, panders, and swindlers, those who succeed through ill-gotten gains. Preferring the company of outlaws on earth, she goes little among the honest and dignified deities of Rome, except when they call her to judgment after she cons nobles and priests out of their estates while in the guise of an elegant priestess. For her defense she shape-shifts, saying, "But I swore by my body, and look, I have no body." She further declares, "I swore by my head, and look, I have no head." Statues made of Laverna show either a head or a body, but never both at the same time, so she will always have an out. The poet Virgil calls her "the craftiest and most knavish" of all beings. She delights in upsetting the status quo and confounding the righteous.

Once an underworld goddess of the mysterious Etruscans, Laverna becomes the goddess of thieves because of her association with the darkness thieves prefer. Though a victim of a crime may call out to her for revenge, she is not often venerated by solid citizens. Yet, she has a sanctuary on Rome's Aventine Hill, near Porta Lavernalis, the city gate named after her. Laverna's temples are most often found in groves where robbers pray for success and where they go to divide their loot afterward. Libations to her are poured with the left hand, considered the crafty or contrary hand. Playing cards are used in her rites. She rewards those who are successful in their knavery, and disdains those who are caught. She is worshiped in the language of secrets and in the purest silence. The poet Horace reports of one who whispers to her, "Give me the art of cheating and deceiving, of making men believe that I am just," and is thus revealed as an imposter and infiltrator.

When Laverna appears:

Think outside the box. Draw outside the lines. The situation cannot be met head on without encountering trouble, so think of another way. Distract, circumvent, cajole; whatever works.

Cause people to question the assumptions they have about you. Redefine yourself. Strive for more freedom in your thoughts and behavior. Be prepared for a shake-up if you have been assuming too much or relying too heavily on the status quo.

This is a good time to work for yourself, your benefit, your own best interests. Keep an eye out. Your partners, coworkers, employees, or employers may be honest, but their interests have diverged from yours.

In silence and darkness, you may find the answer that has been eluding you.

Eight of Air — Crow Mother
Hopi Goddess of Initiation

Take responsibility to break through restriction.

The Hopi Crow Mother (Angwusnasomtaka) is revered as the mother of all kachinas, the spirits that make up the natural world—spirits of living beings as well as the ancestors who have become part of nature. Kachinas have powers of rainfall, protection, and healing that the people desire, while they enjoy prayer feathers, corn pollen, and respect. Hopi rituals are mutual gift-giving ceremonies that preserve harmony in the world.

Crow Mother appears on the mesas at the first full moon of spring, initiating the yearly Powamu ceremony of purification and renewal. She comes from the San Francisco Mountains carrying a basketful of bean sprouts to the village, symbolizing new life for the community. When she comes, she sings the song of the kachinas and their coming to this land.

Crow Mother teaches the proper way to live in community. She presides over the initiation rites of Hopi children at the age of nine or ten, instructing them in the ways of the people. She reveals the secret that the mysterious and powerful kachinas who appear among them are their elders, masked and costumed. Shown behind Crow Mother are her whips, made from the blades of the yucca plant. They stand between her and the child's return home. The children do not yet know that home will not be the same, because they will have changed. The initiate will be whipped, four strokes, the only time in their lives the children are ever beaten. They must face their fear, they must face surprising pain, and they must accept knowledge and the shattering of their childhood illusions. When they do, they are rewarded with a prayer feather and a meal. Then the new young adults are reunited with their community and welcome to join the sacred kiva societies.

When Crow Mother appears:

You are not strengthened by remaining isolated.

To step out of a stuck situation, you need to step up. Face what has been holding you back. Recognize the truth when you hear it. Self-centered and childish fancies impede your participation in a larger world.

Learn the lessons offered by the situation. It will take some discipline, but your future need not be colored by old disappointment or current disillusionment.

Create a prayer stick. Find a stick on a walk. Wrap it with colored yarn, using from one to four colors, repeating your intention with each winding. Tie on stones, shells, and feathers. Give the prayer stick to the earth and sky by leaving it outside in a special place. Leave it, walk away, and do not look back. Trust your prayer will be heard.

Nine of Air — Banshee
Irish Spirit of Prophecy

If you would know, do not fear to see.

The Banshee wails in the mists, chilling the heart with her cries, prophesying the doom of times great and small. Her name comes from the Irish Bean Sidhe, pronounced like banshee and meaning Fairy Woman. She is also called Bean Chaointe (Keening Woman), whose howl can shatter glass.

The Banshee sees visions of worlds beyond this one. She knows the fairy realms and the land of the dead. Her knowledge is old, potent, and dark. Traditionally, a Bean Sidhe attends the five ancient Irish families, such as the O'Briens and the O'Neills, but the list varies depending on who tells the tale. For her clan, the Fairy Woman will advise on the outcome of their battles and keen for the death of their chiefs. There are several prophets believed to be incarnate banshees. In 1437, an Irish seer tells King James I of Scotland of his impending murder.

When she appears, she wears many guises. She is the beautiful, pale, young woman wrapped in a shroud. She is the decrepit old woman dressed in rags covered in graveyard dust. She is the washerwoman, washing the bloody clothing or armor of those about to die. She may be a hooded crow or a hare or a stoat, the familiars of Irish witches. Often only the Banshee's keen can be heard. It may be a soft, otherworldly tune. A screech of protest against injustice. She may scream with the torture of innocents in her voice. Some say she delights in driving her hearers insane, or driving them to become reckless or frightened into finding their deaths. Yet others say the Banshee does not cause death but comes only to warn that fate is near, so that her hearers may learn from it, act on it, and prepare to face it.

When the Banshee appears:

Fear is getting in the way of seeing the truth of the situation. Recognize them, but do not give your fears priority when making a big decision.

Prophecy, the true seeing of the future, is possible at this time. Separate what you wish for, what you dread, and what you expect, in order to see clearly. Look also for the things that do not seem to fit in any of these categories. This represents something for which your mind currently has no context, so it performed a substitution. Dig deeper to let more emerge.

Things that well up in dark places within you can come from a very old place, beyond an accessible cause or reason. Feel it for what it is. Do not make it into something it is not because it is difficult to define.

Try keening to give the darkness some expression. Moan, screech, and wail. Do not keep silent and still with your pain.

Ten of Air — Erinyes
Greek Goddess of Punishment

Endure it or end it.

The Erinyes, the Strong Ones, are more commonly known as the Furies. Clad in the short skirts, boots, and skins of a huntress, and with serpents in their hair, the Greek goddesses of vengeance and retribution are usually found at work in the underworld applying the scourge. It is their sacred duty to punish the souls of the damned. At other times the Erinyes may be called forth to the upper world to inflict disease, suffering, and reason-destroying madness upon an evildoer. An Orphic hymn speaks of them thus, "Revenge and sorrows dire to you belong, hid in a savage vest, severe and strong."

Born of the blood of castrated Uranus, the usurped father god, the Erinyes avenge crimes against the natural order. These include disrespect of the gods, violation of the law of hospitality, and, most especially, murders and offenses against the laws of kinship and the sanctity of family. A victim of a crime who seeks justice can call down the curse of the Erinyes upon the perpetrator, though if one would do so, one had best be free of such misconduct oneself.

Some say the wrath of the Furies may be placated by ritual purification and specific atonements. Others say the goddesses cannot be stopped by tears, pleading, or sacrifice once their righteous anger is aroused. Yet, one may hope to avert their gaze from minor infractions with offerings of black sheep, white doves, or narcissus flowers.

The Erinyes pursue the matricide Orestes, driving him mad, but are called off by Olympian decree. Rightly livid, decrying the betrayal of the younger gods, they are supposedly consoled and their fury redirected by Athena's promises of sacrifices and honor. They are given a new name, the Eumenides, the Kindly Ones, in the hope that their rage will be appeased.

When the Erinyes appear:

Whether deserved or not, hard times are at hand. Now you know the worst. Get up and get along as best you can, perhaps trying a different road as you do.

Beseech the gods or surrender to fate. A power greater than you can direct or control is in play in the situation. It is possible that a power greater than you may set you free or give you strength.

Purify yourself. Expose yourself to a hard wind and let it whip away your regrets. Pare yourself down to the bone to start anew.

If you have done someone wrong, apologize. Make restitution if possible.

If someone has done you wrong, either let it go to set yourself free, or set yourself upon a path of righteous vengeance, one that punishes the wicked, not the innocent.

Amazon of Air — Skadi
Norse Goddess of Winter and Hunting

Hone the skills that lead to freedom.

Skadi is the beautiful goddess of winter in the northern land of Scandinavia, a land named for her. Her name means Shadow, for only winter has the power to darken the sun so. Wearing a short hunting dress and fur leggings, she dashes through the icy mountains on the skis she invented, bearing her sharp spear and piercing arrows and accompanied by her beloved wolves.

A strong and ancient giantess, Skadi storms Asgard, home of the Norse gods, after they cause the death of her father. All of them together cannot withstand her might, and the gods offer her anything in their power to give if she will stop attacking them. She demands just two things. The gods must make her laugh and let her choose a husband from their company, for she is hot blooded and has been alone long enough.

The trickster god Loki makes her laugh by tying his testicles to the beard of a billy goat for a ridiculous and painful tug of war. To select her mate, Skadi's eyes are blindfolded, and she is allowed to feel the legs of all the gods. She chooses the most shapely calves, believing them to belong to the beautiful god Baldur. But they are the legs of the ocean god Njord. Accepting her choice, she goes to live with him in the sea.

Skadi is unhappy away from her snowy home, in a place where all is drippy and gray instead of white and sparkling. The couple decide to take turns alternating their time between the mountains and the shore, but both are miserable this way. They separate amicably, since Skadi finds she prefers her original independent existence to this contrived and incompatible marriage. Skadi returns to her snowy peaks and soon finds her true mate, the god of winter Ulle, by choosing to live uncompromised in the place and manner she loves and is suited for.

When Skadi appears:

Independence requires authenticity, not isolation. Yet, being self-sufficient keeps you true. There is joy in discovering how capable you can become.

Stand up for what you believe in. Believe in yourself most of all. Believe in your rights and your right to a life of your choosing. Believe in your value. Believe in your ability to make change happen.

Seeing clearly what is not going to work for you can save you a lot of time. Say no to a proposition that takes you completely out of your element and away from your sources of strength. A singular challenge is one thing; an endless struggle is another.

Adding levity is not foolish. Unrelieved seriousness leads to bad decisions.

Siren of Air—Lilith
Babylonian Goddess of Darkness

Be seduced by the strange to grow your mind.

Lilith spreads her shadow over her own origins: She is Sumerian and Babylonian; she is Jewish and European. She is a powerful goddess, a spirit of the wind, an evil succubus. Her oldest known titles include Maid of Desolation and Maiden of Darkness. Lil means wind or spirit. Sexual female demons called *lilitu* appear in Sumerian writings from 3000 BCE onward. In Christian and Jewish medieval folklore, Lilith is a sexual vampire, a succubus, delighting in the defilement of men by causing them wet dreams.

Lilith the winged storm demon represents the goddess Inanna's fears that she must conquer in the Sumerian tale of the Huluppu Tree. This is a sacred tree that Inanna plants in her garden and tends until she comes of age, when she must cut it down to make her bed and throne. But the Dark Maid has made her home in the tree trunk, her bird has made a nest in its branches, and her snake has curled among its roots. In Hebrew legend, Lilith is called Night Owl and Screech Owl. She refuses to have sex beneath Adam and is cursed to give birth to one hundred demon children each day. Both of these stories end with her fleeing into the desert to find peace.

Even in a single ancient depiction, Lilith defies a simple definition. With her wings, taloned feet, and dire owl companions, she is a demon of the night, reflecting the mysteries of dream and death. Her jewels and her crown, the shugurra crown of the steppe composed of multiple horns, are all symbols of the Queen of Heaven and Earth. Her frontal nakedness sings with the power of sexuality and fertility. The rod and rings in her hands speak of universal laws and principles. Her gaze is direct; her hands are uplifted in a holy gesture. She holds sway over realms of violence, fear, and mystery. She holds sovereignty over sexuality and all forces of nature, over the complete, magical processes of life and death.

When Lilith appears:

In darkness, fears and monsters multiply. Use your imagination to entertain yourself, not harm yourself. Know where you are pushing the boundaries about what is reasonable, even while knowing that some things will never make sense.

In darkness, power hides. Know it, face it, release it, work it. Quit hiding from yourself all that you are and all that you feel. It is time to quit compromising your soul.

Dark desires do not have to be acted out in illicit ways to be useful for creation or motivation. Denial does not illuminate the darkness.

In this world, sex and death come intertwined. They exist one with another to bring endless variety to life.

Witch of Air—Oya
Santeria Goddess of the Whirlwind

Tear the veil between worlds, and anything can happen.

Oya is the Yoruba and Santería goddess of the whirlwind, the beautiful, violent, fearless daughter of Yemaya, goddess of the sea. She controls the air and the winds. Warrior and horsewoman, she rides storms into battle and wields a beaded horsetail, the Irukere, to stir up lightning. Her name translates to Tearer, the force that rips down to the roots. Oya dances over the earth, twirling in her dress of many colors. She brings change to all she touches. Her power drives the transformation of the world. She is the force of destruction that carries the potential for renewal in its wake.

Known for her fierce passions, Oya is protective of the ones she loves, although she's careless of the chaos she can cause. She is more complex than her energy and ferocity make apparent. She has experienced deep sorrow, but she is not broken by it. Oya gave birth to nine stillborn children. She remembers them through tying colored scarves around her waist, using the sacred cloth that contains every color but black. She journeys to the place of creation, to the holy city of Ife. She dances her prayer for her children's rebirth. She dances in and out of the heart of mystery. She dances up a new world.

Her places of power are places of change and transition. One is the marketplace, where her people gather to exchange the money, goods, and services desired and required by their lives. The marketplace is where Oya oversees the changing of fortunes and the practices of business. Another special place of hers is the gate of a cemetery. She is the guardian of the realm of the ancestors, and the goddess who greets souls as they prepare to enter that realm. Her power moves people from one way of living to another, and from one world to the next.

When Oya appears:

Your power is great during this time of upheaval. Do not become so focused on what you want that you are unaware of collateral damage. Do not let the whirlwind catch you up or knock you down. Find balance through movement and action rather than stasis.

When your nerves feel on edge, do not fall over the line for the release it can provide. The relief will be temporary, the fallout more lasting. Mastery comes from holding the line, riding the storm, and understanding you can make it.

Power comes from knowing your heart, your soul, your center of creation, and from spending time there.

To invite Oya's blessing of renewal into your home or business, set out a colorful bowl where most of the work and energy exchange occur. Fill it with eggplants, plums, and chocolates, things that are sweet, rich, sensual, dark, and juicy.

Hag of Air—Dhumavati
Hindu Widow Goddess

What appears unlucky becomes something sacred.

Dhumavati is the Hindu smoke goddess, the widow goddess. Covered in ash, she dresses in rags gleaned from the cremation grounds. There is a time when she lives with the god Shiva in the Himalayas. She is hungry and asks him for food. When he refuses, she swallows him and widows herself. The widow has a difficult, disrespected social position among her people, but the hunger of the goddess is satisfied only by eating the god who contains the entire world.

Dhumavati is assertive and determined to go her own contrary way. She is associated with the ugly aspects of reality, with hunger, thirst, and need. She represents all that is inauspicious. She is Shakti without Shiva, the goddess without god, a strange figure in the well-paired world of the Hindu. She sits in a cart without a horse, since a widow is thought to have nowhere to go.

Dhumavati is worshiped by widows and bachelors, by people who renounce the world, and by sorcerers and witches. Her companions are the unlucky, unclean carrion and garbage-eating crows, the symbols of black magic and dark forces. She is especially knowledgeable in the use of spells for the ending of things, for death and separation. Her tool is the winnowing basket. With this she separates what is necessary from what is not, what is nourishing from what is deceiving, what is true from what is false. She sees through the smoke of outer forms to comprehend the inner essence. She has the power to take what appears unlucky, sanctify it, and turn it into a blessing.

For Dhumavati is in truth a wisdom goddess. When the seeker overcomes distaste at her ugliness and fear of her misfortune, the goddess becomes a divine teacher who reveals the secrets to obtaining ultimate knowledge beyond all illusion.

When Dhumavati appears:

It is easy to count blessings that everyone recognizes, but not so easy when fortune appears contrary. Look for opportunities to change your perceptions. When something you took as given you now see to be untrue, create a different definition in its place.

Find the hidden blessings in the situation. Claim a weakness as a badge of courage. Set yourself free through acceptance of what is imperfect or strange.

Build a fire big enough to burn something that represents a trauma from your past. Be naked, pure, alone, and focused. Watch the object burn, watch its form become smoke. Smoke can twist around; it can linger or dissipate. Inhale anything you want to keep of the experience. Exhale all you are ready to see gone. If it is necessary, ask for justice on your behalf. Entrust the matter into the hands of the goddess and be done.

Pay attention when crows speak. When you hear them, consider what human illusion they are mocking. Laugh with them when you can. Find crow feathers and set them around your home for luck.

Ace of Earth—Gaia
Greek Goddess of the Earth

The earth gives birth to giants. Time to grow.

Inseparable from her element, Gaia rises from the earth. She eyes the sky and holds up her hands to bless the children around her. Arising from primeval Chaos, the earth of the ancient Greeks is a disk topped by the dome of heaven with the pit of Tartaros below, and the seas and mountains upon her breast.

Gaia is the Mother of All, for everything in nature comes from her flesh, whether animal, tree, or rock. She is the mother of the gods as well. They descend from her union with another elemental from the dawn of creation, Ouranos, the sky above. Gaia is fertility and cannot help but bring forth children. She is nature and cannot help but desire life for them.

It is this last, her having primary loyalty to her children over her mate, that causes conflict with the heavenly gods. Ouranos, in his fear of being supplanted, imprisons several of her children within her womb, causing her extreme pain. After she helps her son Kronos overthrow Ouranos for his oppression, the son betrays her and does the same as the father. She helps another son step up, Zeus, who releases the Titans from her body but confines them to Tartaros in his fear of their strength. Gaia then mates with Tartaros and produces tribes of terrible giants and monsters. These children rise to fight against the upstart and his friends. Gaia supports and bears them all. She does not stop providing life, no matter the circumstances.

Thereafter the young gods name themselves Olympians and claim all powers as their own. But no one, immortal or not, can control or be apart from Gaia's primal being. She provides the place, the means, and the power for all earthly life to happen. Since she alone knows all that takes place upon her body, it is she who whispers deep wisdom to the ancient oracles.

When Gaia appears:

Seek Gaia's wisdom in nature. Hold stones in your hands. Listen to the stirring of leaves and the play of water. Watch the flight of birds. Go to sacred places. If she does not answer in a pertinent or meaningful way, you may need a different question or approach. You may need to give it time. When you practice, you learn what works.

Embracing your life is not a one-time task. For best results, keep your arms open and keep going. Be brave enough to work on your big dream.

Make a vow to make manifest the next idea that contains a seed of something good. It doesn't have to be the greatest or only idea you will ever have. Show you are serious about making things happen, and they will.

Honor the source of your resources. Work to strengthen and repair your connections and relationships where necessary. Without access to resources, you cannot get anywhere.

Two of Earth — Hel
Norse Goddess of the Underworld

If both are the reality, there is no choice.

Sister to wolf and serpent, daughter of a giantess and a divine troublemaker, Hel rules the Norse and Germanic underworld from her hall of Helheim. Welcome in her hall are the souls who do not perish in battle or drown in the sea, but who die due to accident, sickness, or old age. Although some think it inglorious to die so, her hall offers amenities similar to Odin's, Freya's, or Ran's. After death, the soul is cared for as it deserves, as it has earned through one's deeds. And Hel's eyes, hooded as they are, see all.

Hel embodies duality in a world where life and death are two sides of a coin. Her body is half-blackened, rotten, and half-sweet, whole flesh. She is seen both as honored queen of the underworld and as one of the creatures of wickedness intent on overthrowing the gods at the end of the world, when she will call upon her shades to join her army. The way she is seen reflects change in human perception of the land of the dead, from a place of refuge to a place of judgment and then punishment, and stories of Hel grow more fearsome over time, with her dining table named Hunger, and her hall, Ice.

Her unusual appearance is not due to her role as ruler of the dead. She is given her realm because the gods are too disturbed by her gruesome visage to accept her presence among them. She embraces her realm as a place where she can be just who she is, a place where she can say what's what, a place where truth matters more than appearance.

In Hel's underworld, opposites are accepted out of necessity and, through inescapability, are transcended. In Hel, two do not blend into one. Although intimately connected, each retains unique identity. Power lives in the dynamic tension between the two.

When Hel appears:

You have more than one task, more than one voice, more than one passion. You must make choices in your behavior, but do not deny this truth about your life. Beware of people and situations that ask you to renounce parts of yourself. Be willing to see what you are when you stop catering to illusion and denial.

If you face a choice, ask yourself which will be easier to endure. Think long term. Think best-case and worst-case scenarios. See how expectations sway your thoughts and decisions. Let what should be done coalesce out of the options at hand. Don't try to predict its shape. See what becomes solid. See what can be made real.

Do not stay wounded. Grow over and grow around the pain, and move on. Let dead things stay buried. There is less treasure to be found digging in the past than embracing opportunity in the present.

Your hands may be full, but you are more capable than you know. Do not be reluctant to take on another project if you see it has great potential. Giving a little of yourself every day adds up to accomplishment over time.

Three of Earth—Norns
Norse Goddesses of Destiny

Small stitches weave the world. Do your part.

The Norns, the goddesses of fate for Norse and Germanic peoples, are three crones or maidens who live among the roots of the World Tree, the wondrous ash Yggdrasil. It is their task, their service unto the end of the world, to maintain the health of the tree, drawing water from the Well of Urth to nourish the roots. The health of the tree and the lives of people are intertwined, for the tree contains the worlds that humanity experiences. A wicked dragon lurks below and gnaws at the roots to harry the living.

The Norns are agents of fate and destiny. They shape what will happen through pouring the sacred water, by etching runes into the trunk, and by spinning and weaving. Their names are Urth (What Has Been), Verthandi (What Is Becoming), and Skuld (What Shall Be). They are also called Fate, Being, and Necessity. Fate is associated with the past, not the future, for life is not absolutely predetermined except in its ultimate end. Not even the gods will escape the end of the world.

The Norns set limits to what can be done. They have laid down the primal laws, creating the warp and woof of life itself. It is right for humans to do as much as they can within the boundaries that have been determined. Fate is what one must suffer, but it is also what one may achieve, and the obligation and necessity to attempt it. Free will and the potential for individual action exist because the tapestry of the Norns is not yet complete, but this also means that confusion and uncertainty must still exist as well.

Destiny is following the path, step by step, stitch by stitch, that leads to doing as the Norns inscribe, helping to weave the greater tapestry and nourish the living tree through one's everyday acts.

When the Norns appear:

Now is not the time to rush or skip steps, lest the final result be less strong, beautiful, and useful than it may otherwise be. Do it right the first time.

Cooperative efforts bring success. What you struggle to do may be a job for someone who can embrace it. Offering what you have and can do may be a blessing to another. Look for opportunities to share your skills.

Beware of saboteurs of your abilities and your work. Do not feed the dragons through conflict or doubt. Hum a lullaby, keep them calm or distracted, and keep doing what you do.

Write down what you want to happen as if it has already occurred. Handwrite it, using a magical or beautiful script. Be wise with your wishes. Make one for you, one for another, and one for the Tree. See how, in the story you create of your life, goodness can grow from what you do.

Four of Earth — Sphinx
Greek Monster of Fate

How you define your life limits your life.

The Sphinx is a fearsome, fourfold creature, having the head of a woman, the wings of an eagle, the body of a lion, and a serpent-headed tail. She is one of a family of winged demons, like the Furies and Harpies, who ravage the living at the bidding of the Greek gods. She plagues the outskirts of the town of Thebes as punishment for an ancient crime. She challenges all who travel the road to solve her riddle: What creature walks on four legs in the morning, two legs at midday, and three legs in the evening? The answer encompasses the entirety of a human life from infancy to old age. Those who do not understand the answer—that she asks them to define and claim their own life—are killed.

As well as "strangler," the literal meaning of her name, the Sphinx is called "prophesying maiden." Votive sphinxes are offered at Delphi, the center of prophecy in the ancient world, where the priestesses also speak in sacred riddles. It is the oracle at Delphi that sets spinning the events of Thebes, when she tells of the son who will kill his father and marry his mother. It prompts the father to abandon the child. Years later, it prompts the same child to leave his adopted home and encounter his birth father. By speaking the prophecy, the oracle becomes the instrument of fate.

A large marble sculpture of the Sphinx faces the inner sanctum of Delphi. She guards the omphalos, the sacred stone egg that marks the center of the world, the heart of the oracle's power. The Sphinx also guards the peace of the dead. Sculptures of the monster are often found on tombstones and within temple grounds, there to frighten those who would defile the dead through coveting their grave goods and special treasures.

The deeper answer to the riddle includes this fourth and final stage. Life is about more than what one possesses. It is about what one leaves behind.

When the Sphinx appears:

Definitions work two ways, helping you understand reality and separating your perception from reality. Upholding or debating rigid definitions can require endless vigilance. Find your own reality, the only position you must defend, and find the center of your power.

Write down four pillars of your situation, things that appear fated, concrete, or absolute. One by one, redefine them. Rewrite them in words that allow for creativity and transformation. Rewrite them in words that question or embellish their necessity.

Honor what you have to work with in this one sacred lifetime: your body, your mind, your heart, and your external resources. Be disciplined with what you should be using better. Be careful with what you should respect more. Protect your resources from greed and abuse.

Look ahead. Your story will end someday. Where it will end and how it will be remembered are written through actions in the present.

Five of Earth — Demeter
Greek Goddess of Agriculture

Give no part of yourself to what does not sustain you.

Demeter is the Olympian goddess of agriculture and grain, the sustainer of humanity. She is the goddess of the fertile earth. In early times the secrets of that fertility are known to her alone. Her power of agriculture is shared only after she suffers a terrible loss and undergoes a painful journey.

Her daughter, Persephone, disappears. Demeter is distraught and searches the earth from the fields of sunrise to the islands of the west. She does not eat. She does not wash. Her shining robes turn to rags. When she discovers that the lord of the underworld took her child, and the father god Zeus allowed it, her hot grief turns to stone-cold rage. She turns her back on Mount Olympus and the gods.

Demeter wanders the earth again, no longer searching but still suffering. She arrives in the town of Eleusis. The people cannot see she is a goddess, ragged and shrouded as she is, but they see she is noble and in need. She is welcomed kindly and offered food, although the harvest has not been good. For as Demeter hurts, so does the earth. Nothing grows but famine while she knows agony. Zeus, worried the mortals will die and sacrifices cease, sends the gods to entreat her. She refuses. She will not restore the fertility of the earth until she can hold her daughter again. Zeus and Hades finally accede to her one demand. Persephone will return and the land will bear fruit again.

Before Demeter leaves her life in Eleusis, she reveals to the people the secrets of a fertile earth and teaches the way of her worship. Her mysteries are of seed and soul, each in its time. The gift of her grain provides prosperity while on earth. The gift of her mysteries promises a blessed afterlife to come.

When Demeter appears:

Accept that fallow times are part of the cycle of fertility. Sometimes nothing is the best thing to do. When nothing is all you can do, get through as best you can. Know that fallow is not final. Opportunity for change comes with the change in seasons.

Be strong, but not so tough you do not recognize comfort when it is offered by another.

Release expectation of what you may receive for your efforts. Thoughts of disappointment or reward will interrupt the authenticity of a process that is far from completion. Stay present with your reality as it unfolds.

Refuse to be complicit in selfishness or wickedness. Do not give energy to those who will abuse it. Learn the power of saying no. If you find it difficult, practice on small things that are not so fraught. You need not be impolite or uncaring. "No" informs yourself and others of your priorities.

Six of Earth — Tsonokwa

Kwakiutl Wild Woman of the Woods

Measure wealth by giving.

In the rainforests of the Pacific Northwest lives Tsonokwa, the Wild Woman of the Woods. She can be dreadful to encounter, a hairy black giantess with pendulous breasts and red pursed lips. Another name for her is Whistling Woman, and another, Wealth Giver, for the riches the forest holds. Her call is the sound of wind blowing through the cedars. Her call is the sound of a grandmother's voice. She calls out, luring unsuspecting and greedy children to wander off into the forest. She offers treats. She whispers of boxes of treasure to be found in her home. Children are warned not to take things from her, though, since she will catch and eat them when she can. Which is not often, since she is clumsy and slow and sees poorly.

Though she will stumble around the fire in the wrong direction during the dances, as bestower of wealth Tsonokwa is called upon during potlatch ceremonies to oversee the giveaway of the host's possessions. A person shows their wealth not by having but through giving. Generosity is valued above all. It is what makes a person great. A family will work for a year to hold a splendid feast for a special occasion, with lovely gifts for everyone who attends. The practice of the potlatch redistributes wealth and builds bonds of reciprocity within the community.

Tsonokwa herself gives her riches freely only when someone helps her son. One day, her giant boy is killed by hunters. A poor orphan wandering in the woods finds the body and does not run from the terrible sight. He follows Tsonokwa's call to find her, to lead her to her son. He helps her carry him to her home. She pours water over her son's body from her ever-flowing basin to bring him back to life. She pours water over the orphan, and he grows handsome and strong. Further, Tsonokwa teaches the orphan the secret of the basin, and he revives his parents with her magical water.

When Tsonokwa appears:

Face the challenge in front of you with a courageous and generous heart, and your fortunes will be renewed.

Laziness will eat your power. Greed will eat your heart. Attach no strings to gifts given or received, only bonds of mutual respect or affection. Give and receive with grace, without self-importance or mortification. Recognize your wealth. Recognize its source. Every living person is given more from the earth than it is possible to give back, so be humble, grateful, and generous whenever possible.

From the western red cedar, the peoples of the Pacific Northwest receive wood for their homes, their fires, their boats (for fishing, transportation, and trade), their tools. Strips of the inner bark are woven into clothing, baskets, and blankets. The tree's gifts provide the entire material foundation of their lives. There is currently a resource in your life that you are underutilizing. Take inventory of what you have. Attention to craftsmanship will help you do more.

Seven of Earth — Ereshkigal
Sumerian Goddess of the Underworld

The oldest roots grow in the deepest places.

Ereshkigal is the Sumerian goddess of death and queen of the underworld. She is known mostly through Inanna's story of descent and resurrection. Though Inanna suffers when she journeys below, it is due to her trespassing, not because the underworld is a place of punishment.

Ereshkigal's realm is a spiritual place that opens up for the dead after their burial. It is their proper place, as the heavens are the proper place of the gods. Those who are dying pray for the Lady of the Great Place to receive them, and that they may be fortunate enough to find a place near her feet and never wander lost upon the earth. In the well-ordered universe of Sumer, the underworld has rules even the gods must obey:

- No one may return to the land of the living.
- No one may rule both Above and Below.

Though in Inanna's descent she surrenders her possessions at each of the seven gates as required, she tries to break these two fundamental laws.

The same inexorable rules brought Ereshkigal her crown. Once she was a beautiful maiden beloved by the gods, before she is taken from heaven by the dragon of the underworld to be his bride. Enki, the god of wisdom, pursues, battles, and kills the serpent. But his magic cannot restore Ereshkigal to the land of the living. Instead she accepts the throne of the realm below. She takes the Great Bull of Heaven (Taurus) for her husband and seven galla, lesser serpents of the underworld, as her servants.

In this image, Ereshkigal receives her reptilian features and fertility characteristics from a Mesopotamian funerary figurine one thousand years older than the cities of ancient Sumer. Many similar statuettes have been found, all buried carefully next to someone's beloved dead. The dead were given back to the embrace of the earth in a time when Ereshkigal and Inanna were not rivals, and Above and Below not so separated.

When Ereshkigal appears:

Intuitive leaps are the result of powerful but subterranean processes. Trust the one that emerges from the depths over the one coming at you from left field.

Though the consequences may not be apparent or just, certain rules cannot be broken and some should not be broken. Know which are which. Success does not come from intemperate or injudicious action.

Symbols can lose meaning, and omens become lost if attention is not paid. Keeping a record over time reveals patterns at work. Discoveries await you. Keep digging.

When magical tools have lost their power and purity, recharge them by burial in the earth for seven days before cleansing and reconsecration.

Eight of Earth—Cailleach
Scottish Goddess of Winter

The mountain is built stone by stone.

The Cailleach (pronounced *KY-loch* or *KA-loch*) is the hag of winter, the mother of the gods, and the goddess of mountains, rocks, and cold, bare earth. In Scotland, weather comes from the high peaks, for storm clouds build up among them. From there, winter spreads across the countryside. Cailleach means veiled or hooded, like a mountain wrapped in mist.

A blue-skinned, cyclopean giantess, the Cailleach strides across the mountaintops on her yearly journey across the land from the Irish to the North Sea. Rocks fall from her apron to become stony hills and great boulders. She washes the plaid across her shoulders in a great whirlpool on the west coast to signal the end of summer and the beginning of her reign as winter's queen. The next day the land is covered in snow. Her hair is brushwood, her face the color of cold, deep sky. Her single eye shows her power to see time and space at a different level, more as tools than constraints. She looks past things too small for her to notice. She builds stone by stone but on a grand scale. She makes mountains. She builds a homeland.

The red deer of the mountains are called the cattle of the Cailleach. Hers is an ancient world of hunters and of deer—not cattle. She gathers her deer and guides them to protected vales at the onset of winter. Similarly, she offers shelter to careful travelers. For others, she calls up a storm and allows them to perish. The Cailleach has a thrice-knotted rope that holds her power over the winds. If she loosens one knot, a breeze blows. The second knot, and a stiff wind sweeps over the hills. Should she untie the third knot, a blasting gale will set the pines crashing and her stones tumbling down the mountain.

When the Cailleach appears:

Work steadily. Work in proved and respectful ways. There is no cheating on this path. There are no shortcuts to a lasting achievement.

You may well be rewarded in other ways, but let the work itself be valuable to you. Your efforts should bring you strength, not depletion.

Keep an eye on the larger picture. Look at where your daily steps are taking you. See where making an adjustment to a routine might take you somewhere better.

Try traditional cord magic. As late as the fourteenth century, Scottish weather witches sold knotted cords openly to sailors, so the seamen could unloose the knots as they needed wind. Choose a cord in a color and material that feels right. Choose a time and a place appropriate to the power you wish to store for a later need. Call on the power until you feel giant inside. Chant as you tie the knots. "Knot of one, spell's begun. Knot of two, spell comes true. Knot of three, so mote it be."

When releasing the power, either all at once or over three consecutive days, untie the knots in the same order as you tied them. The last knot released is the climax, the final and most powerful knot tied in the previous ritual.

Nine of Earth — Blodeuwedd
Welsh Goddess of Flowers

Enjoy the sweet season while it lasts.

Blodeuwedd (usually pronounced *BLOD-ay-weth*), "Flower Face," is the Welsh goddess of flowers, of the earth in the bloom of spring. Blodeuwedd's story appears in the Mabinogion, tales of ancient magic translated in the nineteenth century from medieval Welsh manuscripts. The lovely maiden is conjured by the magician Gwydion, uncle of Llew Llaw Gyffes, to be the sun hero's bride. She is fashioned from the buds and blossoms of nine flowers, nine powers of tree and herb: chestnut for longevity (shown on her dress), meadowsweet for grace (her yoke), nettle for practicality (her necklace), broom for vitality (her hair), oak for power (her eyebrows), corn cockle for pride (her mouth), bean for soul (her nose), and primrose for enchantment (her eyes), with the sacred hawthorn crowning her as Queen of the May (her cap).

Blodeuwedd is content with the life she's given until Llew goes on a journey, leaving her on her own for the first time. She promptly finds and falls in love with another man, a fine hunter. She and her lover plot to kill her immortal husband. She uses craft and cunning to discover the only way he can be slain. Instead of dying, however, Llew becomes an eagle and flies away. Gwydion restores Llew's humanity, avenging him by changing Blodeuwedd into an owl, that she may forever call out in the night for her lost life and lost love.

Her story may seem to be a morality tale about infidelity, or maybe that of a woman coming to self-realization and rebelling against a life defined by another. Truly, it is mythic, the ancient tale of the changing seasons. Blodeuwedd's lovers are the gods of summer and winter, eternal rivals for her favor. Though in another season the earth goddess may be mother or crone, Blodeuwedd is the goddess in her May aspect, the maiden of the beautiful, blossoming time, the goddess of the powers of bud and blossom, of tree and herb. The owl she will become sleeps on a branch behind her. Its time is not yet here.

When Blodeuwedd appears:

Recognize all the powers that are part of you, the events, the people, and the talents that have made you what you are. Name your powers. Name nine of them. Find a representation for each one that you might plant in a garden, set on a special shelf, or sew or knit into clothing or accessories.

Assert your intention to direct and star in your own life. The longer you allow yourself only a supporting role, the less meaningful your story.

The ephemeral is most precious; embrace it or you miss it. The treasure of a flower exists in a single, blissful inhalation. Let the magic of flowers help your healing, in essences and elixirs, in fresh scents, and in beautiful, full vases. The death of the flower makes way for the fruit.

Improve your estate. Invest in your home and in your dreams. Focus on what you need to build a beautiful life for yourself.

Ten of Earth — Ala
Igbo Goddess of the Ground

Kin and kind, living and dead, all are part of one another.

Ala, also known as Ana, is the goddess of the ground for the Igbo people of Nigeria. For the Igbo, all ground is holy ground because it is all Ala. She is the totality of the earth in all its variety and appearances, from lush growth to the emptiness of fallow fields. She is there at the beginning of life, and she is there at the end. She makes the baby grow in the mother. She takes the souls of the dead into her own womb.

Wood or mud statues of Ala are painted in bright colors and are housed in temples or set in the center of the village. The goddess, the ancestors, and the earth are ever present and always acknowledged. The statues show Ala as a beautiful Igbo woman, with a long torso and long, thick neck.

The majority of her people are small farmers, in intimate relationship with the land. Their staple crop is the yam. Their fields are so fruitful they export food to neighboring peoples. The yam festival is the party of the year, celebrated with joyful dancing and colorful pageantry, and honoring Ala as earth, goddess, and harvest,. The powerful python is venerated as her messenger, and the fertile crescent moon is her symbol.

Ala is also the goddess of morality and judgment, the keeper of the customs and laws of her people, since all the people's actions take place upon her ground. If someone breaks a taboo of the community, one has also insulted Ala and might immediately be swallowed whole by the earth. Everyone in the community has to respect the laws of Ala, because all live on her, and all suffer if Ala suffers. Creating a good and abundant life is a communal responsibility, working in harmony with what the ground gives.

When Ala appears:

If there is bad blood between you and another, this is a good time to make peace. Let the relationship be honest, neither idealized nor denied. Let your encounter be respectful and straightforward. If the other has transgressed too severely, let the relationship go. Leave the other to Ala. Do not seek vengeance; seek people who are trustworthy.

If you have had good fortune, this is a good time to celebrate it. Gather friends and family for a feast. Buy things of value for your home and gifts for your loved ones. Buy from your community. Support people whose work you admire. Include the less fortunate in your giving.

Put your hands on the bare earth. Feel the immensity opening up beneath them. Everything is there beneath you, and all around you. The past and the future, the dead and the unborn. The power to bring forth all things time and again. Feel this power swell up into own hands, and know what you can make, what you can give.

Renew this basic connection with the earth on a regular basis. With hands and feet and more. Remember where your life comes from and where your life is lived.

Amazon of Earth — Artemis
Greek Goddess of Wild Animals

Vile is the one who would discipline the innocent.

"Artemis of the wilderness, lady of wild beasts ... lion among women ... you hunt down the ravening beasts in the mountains" (Homer's *Iliad*, ca. 800 BCE). Where the wilderness is a terrifying place, Artemis is at her most powerful. Goddess of the hunt, she runs tirelessly through forests of fir and pine with her band of huntresses and her pack of dogs. She dances with her companions among the trees at night. She is bold in the chase, by day or night. No prey on which she sets her sights, whether swift stag or fierce boar, escapes her arrows. But like any good hunter, she does not kill mothers or their young.

Artemis delights in the young of every wild creature, all creatures born with wildness and purity. She is their patron and their protector. She is invoked during childbirth along with Hera, the goddess of marriage, who protects the mother. Artemis protects the newly born. As such, she is a goddess of initiation, called upon for blessing and assistance at the start of a brand-new life. She is called upon by midwives, for not only does she understand the efficacy of certain forest herbs, but immediately after her own holy birth, she leaps to reduce her mother's suffering and helps deliver her own twin brother, the young Apollo.

Artemis protects infants, the most vulnerable of living beings. She guards all innocence and purity, including that of springs and streams of clear water. She guards the immaculate in herself and others as well. Her companions must be as she is, unconquered by romantic love, and under no obligation to anyone except the goddess and the wild land. Her punishment of transgressors is always swift, severe, and usually ultimate, whether those transgressors are her attendants for a lack of chastity, or hunters who would approach her, her wilderness, or her creatures without the respect she deems necessary for the pure and the vulnerable to thrive.

When Artemis appears:

Purify the space you live in. Use the resins and oils of evergreens for aromatics. Clean it energetically and physically. Clear out something you no longer care for but have kept due to nostalgia or obligation. Make your home into a place where your true self shines.

Purify the environment you live in. Go for a walk and pick up trash. Go for a walk instead of drive. Plant and care for trees. Use fewer products that are manufactured. Take steps to travel more swiftly and lightly upon the earth.

Care for the little ones. Defend those who cannot defend themselves. Teach strength through example.

Make sure that companions in your venture share your most-important values. Do not be pressured into a compromise your spirit cannot tolerate.

Shun the bullies, prosecute the trespassers, and do not be intimidated by potential conflict. Stay strong, but most of all, stay free.

You have weapons at your disposal. Aim carefully, shoot with a true heart, and you will achieve your goal.

Siren of Earth—Baubo
Greek Bawdy Goddess

This is life in the body: raw, ridiculous, sublime.

Baubo, also called Iambe, is the goddess of the belly laugh. She takes part in Demeter and Persephone's story, a story of sex and death, fertility and renewal, the story upon which the great Eleusinian Mysteries were based. She represents the power of laughter to activate the power in sexuality, the power of creation.

Baubo, a woman of Eleusis, welcomes Demeter into her home; Demeter, who has wandered, dressed in old robes, grief stricken, in search of her daughter. Baubo gives Demeter a seat by the fire and offers her the sacred drink of kykeon, brewed from barley, honey, and pennyroyal. Demeter is unresponsive, remaining disconsolate and silent.

That is, until Baubo begins to tell bawdy jokes. She lifts her skirt and exposes her genitals. She paints a face on her belly. She dances and gestures obscenely. She causes "the holy lady to smile and to laugh and to have a gracious heart" (Homeric hymn to Demeter). Because of the lewd and absurd nature of Baubo's acts, Demeter is momentarily shocked out of her sorrow. Because the jest is not only funny but sympathetic, from woman to woman, the goddess laughs. A belly laugh, the kind that erupts from deep within and then cannot be stopped. With it, Demeter is awakened from her desolation. A renewal of life becomes possible.

During the three days of Thesmophoria, the ancient women-only festival for Demeter, Greek women who normally lived sequestered lives left their homes, made huts out of greenery, and camped out together. After the solemn ritual and communal mourning came clowning, coarse gestures, and foul language. Every one of these steps was considered essential to restore the fertility of the land. Every woman's participation was needed for this service to Demeter, and in so doing they too were revitalized. Once a year, women could express themselves freely, have their sexuality and their bodies belong to themselves alone, and release their pain through laughter and community.

When Baubo appears:

Levity and humor go where rant and reason cannot.

Laugh and smile deliberately, and see if it helps. For a group healing, take turns laughing artificially, making the silliest sounds you can. Keep going around the circle until real laughter overtakes the show.

Explore your sensual body. Move your body in a way that feels good, even if it looks funny. Stretch like a cat. Dance like a genie. Touch and rub and sweat and soak. Find out what feels good, what feels right. Be more whole with yourself, more accepting, more appreciative of what you can feel.

Explore your physicality through outdoor play and games. Go camping. Have a picnic. Hug a tree. Connect to an environment beyond walls. Feel it through your bare skin.

Push the boundaries of social convention and everyday behavior, especially where it constrains you. Be funny, be funny-looking, be outlandish! Because shaking things up can get things done.

Witch of Earth—Inanna
Sumerian Goddess of Fertility

Make magic in partnership with natural forces.

Inanna's stories, rites, and prayers are among the earliest existent writings, pressed into clay over five thousand years ago. She rules love and sexuality, war and the arts of civilization, prosperity and fertility. She is the storehouse, where grain awaits transformation into bread or the seed of new life. She is the rain, the power that sprouts the grain. She is the spirit for battle; she is the desire for sex; she is the potent bond of love. She descends into the underworld and returns to life from death. Her titles include Lady of Infinite Variety and Amazement of the Land.

Her complexity is not contradiction, for the root of all these powers is in the magic and multiplicity of nature, in the forces and urges that engender and maintain an abundant life. In Mesopotamia, where the art of agriculture began, Inanna's body is one with the arable land. She is the source of all riches. But she needs stimulation from her beloved to bring them forth.

In the card image, based upon a twenty-second-century BCE stone seal, Inanna sits within a bower beneath her emblem, an eight-petal rosette. She wears the crown of the plain, the crown of divinity, formed of layered animal horns. She welcomes her lover, a crowned and sceptered god emerging from the sacred tree. Her desire calls him, that he may join with her in the rite of sacred marriage. To plow her body as the farmer plows the land, to excite her fertility and her pleasure, to bring abundance to the land. In the sacred marriage, primal forces are channeled through honored traditions to serve the life of the land and her people. In her turn, Inanna bestows power on her beloved, sharing with him the authority to order the land and lead the people to greater prosperity.

When Inanna appears:

Learn your plant allies and integrate them into your daily life. Let research narrow the field, then let experience and enjoyment be your guide. Whether through foods, teas, tinctures, or oils, certain plants offer special benefits for your individual biochemistry. Try not to overload your body while you are learning, lest you become unable to sense the sometimes subtle alignments.

Baker or dressmaker, shopkeeper or gardener, if you feel inspired to create or distribute natural goods, the time is propitious for you to embrace your passion. Do not neglect, however, the formalities required for a strong foundation. Also do not neglect to express tangible gratitude to the providing earth.

With the right partner, great good can be achieved. Mutual care and the timely fulfillment of clearly expressed expectations lead to success. Partner only with someone who understands this.

A magical life is a matter of intention, then a matter of reality. Approach everyday tasks with a sense of service, add beauty and meaning to your environment, and connect with other living powers, whether tree or cat. Soon you will see how the world hums and flows, and you will see how you can make your world grow.

Hag of Earth — She Who Watches
Chinook Stone Chief

Remember history, or more will be lost.

Tsagaglalal, who is known as She Who Watches, is the chief of a peaceful, populous, and prosperous people. For thousands of years, life is good for the people of the many villages around Celilo Falls, where the Columbia River cascades from the high desert of the Great Basin into the lush gorge and on toward the sea. The salmon return each year to leap into their nets. Trade in furs, food, and household and sacred goods comes upriver from the peoples of the Pacific Northwest. Skins, meat, and more come downriver from the tribes of the plains. Everyone meets where the river shifts and changes, where the water roars over worn hills of ancient stone. Tsagaglalal stands on a bluff high above the river and watches over them all.

Then Coyote comes singing. Coyote, creator and trickster and fool. The world is going to change, he sings. How will you be a good chief when the world changes? Tsagaglalal replies, I do not know, but I will watch over my people for as long as I can. Coyote hears and then turns her to stone.

The world changes. She Who Watches sees a plague of tiny, invisible beasts eat up the lives of her people, shatter their civilization, and break the hearts of the survivors. A hundred or more years pass, and still she watches. She watches as a dam is built and the waterfalls choke and the bedrock itself is remade. She watches as her remnant village is drowned entire—all that is rescued are a few pieces of etched and painted stone.

Still she watches, although her scattered people must make a journey to come to her now. Still they come, the old ones, the children, and they sit before the old stone chief. They sit in front of She Who Watches, she who has seen life come and seen life go, she who has seen the world change. The people ask Tsagaglalal to see into their lives. To see the suffering they have known, to see the troubles they now face, and to grant them a vision of resolution, wisdom, and strength.

When She Who Watches appears:

Put your trust in what is known to last through the years.

The world is changing. Bear witness to what is happening. Carry the story and pass it along. Carry the memory and honor what came before. Conscience is a responsibility that lasts a lifetime.

There are answers in the past. Dig beneath the surface of what you remember. Look for the seed; look into when and where the trouble began. If your world can be remade, that is where to begin the building. If it cannot be remade, that is where to say goodbye.

Be open to receiving visions. Do not let hope or despair cloud your eyes. Look for the ordinary symbols in your dreams to reveal depth and meaning over time.

Be hard enough to endure. To be strong as a stone, sit in stillness and hold in your hand a special rock you've found along your path. Quietly, calmly, feel its solidity. Feel it gradually warm to your touch. Begin to feel its long, slow life. Even as pressure shapes it, as fire and ice crack it, as water erodes it, it remains. It is still strong.

Dark Goddess Tarot Spreads

SUBSTANCE AND SHADOW

This two-card spread gives a quick, incisive look into everyday challenges.

1. The Substance.
What is the necessity, the reality, the nitty-gritty of the situation?
What action is required?

2. The Shadow.
What is not concrete yet affects the situation?
What is the hidden influence at work?

WHAT, WHY, AND HOW

This spread offers specific insight into a murky situation or ongoing problem.

1. What is going on with this?

2. Why am I responding like this?

3. How can I change this?

GODDESS BE WITH YOU

This is a spread to orient to one's true self.

(If you are right-handed:)

1. Who stands at your left hand? What helps you understand your experience?
2. Who stands at your right hand? What helps you accomplish your work in the world?

(If you are left-handed:)

1. Who stands at your left hand? What helps you accomplish your work in the world?
2. Who stands at your right hand? What helps you understand your experience?

3. Who has your back? Where do you find protection?
4. Who is leading the way forward? Where do you find inspiration?
5. Who is emerging from your deep self? What is your potential?

Summary
The Journey of the *Dark Goddess Tarot*

On a dark and rainy night in Portland, Oregon, in December 2011, I attended a simple, powerful, public ritual invoking the goddess Hekate. Hekate of the Threshold, Hekate of the Crossroads, Hekate my beloved since 1985. Afterward—in the tradition of cakes and ale, but in this case, fries and a chocolate shake in a pub down the street from the bookstore—my friend and I chatted about magic, ritual, and goddesses. I said that I like the dark goddesses the best, and Bong! went that deep iron bell in my soul. I immediately saw Sedna as the Eight of Cups/Water. I immediately knew this was the project I'd been wanting for so long: the compelling one, the important one, the one that had enough juice to take me through the long journey of its creation. The *Dark Goddess Tarot*.

I got to work, starting with Sedna. I filled my eyes with her stories and with the art of her people. I filled her card with eight of her undersea companions, eight sea creatures important to the Inuit. When I was done, I looked at her and she felt real.

I spent hours researching and drawing every day. I could do this because I'd been unable to find work but had an employed partner, and we'd already done months of belt tightening and making do. But I didn't think, Oh, who might buy this?; I thought, I need to do this.

I started with the suit of Water. I made a list of goddesses with an association with water. I struck off the list any goddess that I felt did not have a dark thread or chord within her. Then I meditated on them until I found a place where their stories connected with Tarot card meanings. Keeping the elemental association was important to me, because it felt important to them, to the goddesses who want to be more present in the world, and more present in people's hearts. Yes, the mourning Demeter could be on the Five of Cups, but she is very much an Earth goddess, so—no. I found another.

What happened as I worked was magical. Once in a while I had written something where it felt like I was transcribing more than creating. This had never happened to me when I was drawing before. But I moved my pencil across the paper and felt not like I was drawing, but like I was revealing. As if I were using the eraser end instead of the lead. Sometimes I didn't get that feeling. Sometimes the drawing still turned out okay. Sometimes I ripped it up and started over.

In March 2013, the drawings were done and I was writing the book, still focused on producing the work but beginning to wonder about the next step, when a friend came to visit from out of state. She wasn't a Tarot or circle friend; she was from the days our little girls were best friends. She looked at my drawings and said that these need to be out there—what would it take to make that happen? I said that self-publishing is the way to make sure it happens, but I don't have the money for a print run. She said that she did, and she wrote me a check. More *Dark Goddess Tarot* magic!

Then—how to turn scanned images and a text document into a Tarot deck? I didn't have the software or the know-how. I could acquire it, and it could be a slow and possibly painful process. Or I could ask another friend for help, someone who had self-published and with whom I'd worked before—Arnell Ando. She was happy to help, and our partnership began. The first edition of the *Dark Goddess Tarot* started shipping in September of 2013. A second printing sold out in March 2018. That might have been the end, since I hadn't the resources for another go. But it seemed as though the goddesses did not want to be lost. They wanted to continue the conversations.

It is October 2019 as I write this, full of gratitude for the good people at Schiffer Books. Through the addition of their work to mine, the *Dark Goddess Tarot* will continue to empower and transform people's lives.